The Broken Body

The Broken Body

JEAN VANIER

DARTON · LONGMAN + TODD

First published in 1988 by
Darton, Longman and Todd Ltd
1 Spencer Court
140–142 Wandsworth High Street
London SW18 4JJ

Reprinted 1988, 1989, 1990, 1992 and 1994

British Library Cataloguing in Publication Data

Vanier, Jean
  The broken body
  1. Christianity, Spiritual Healing
  1. Title
  615.8′52

  ISBN 0-232-51749-5

Phototypeset by Intype, London
Printed and bound in Great Britain by
Page Bros, Norwich

Young people have played an important part in my life over the past twenty years. They are a challenge to me with their deep desire for God and for authentic ways of living the Gospel. But in our broken world such desires cause pain, fear and sometimes despair. This book is for those young people, sometimes angry and rebellious, yet open; sometimes lost, yet searching and thirsting; sometimes weeping, yet maintaining a glimmer of hope.

May it help us to discover the waters flowing from the brokenness of the world and from the heart of Jesus.

Contents

Acknowledgements

I would like to thank, in a special way, Chris Sadler. Her inspiration and insight brought much truth and light and wisdom to this book.

I would also like to thank Teresa de Bertodano, Victoria Wethered and Olive Peat of Darton, Longman & Todd. Their patience and precision have clarified the text and improved the English.

Introduction

This book is written to show a way,
a little way,
that has been given to me
by Jesus,
and to many others all over the world
who are followers of Jesus.
It is a way that is very simple and very healing;
a way that leads us into the love of Jesus
and of his Father,
through a covenant of love
with the poor, the weak and the oppressed.

So many of us flee from people crying out in pain,
people who are broken.
We hide in a world of distraction and pleasure
or in 'things to do'.
We can even hide in various groups of prayer
and spiritual exercises,
not knowing that a light is shining
in the poor, the weak, the lonely and the oppressed.
Or if we do not flee from suffering
perhaps we revolt in anger,
and this, too, blinds us to the light of Jesus
glowing in people who are in pain.

These pages are to tell you,
my brother, my sister,
not to run away from people who are in pain
or who are broken,
but to walk towards them,
to touch them.
Then you will find rising up within you the well of love,
springing from resurrection.

In walking along this way
I have had to meet my own darkness and brokenness
in the deeper knowledge that I am loved,
and so, though I have had to let go
of many dreams for our world
and many illusions about myself,
still I am growing in hope and trust
in the light which shines in each person:
believer or non-believer.
Yes, in that broken child,
a light is shining;
in that man in prison,
a heart is beating;
in that woman, victim of prostitution,
there is a yearning for life;
in the rich and greedy person, seeking power,
there is a child of purity;
in that young man dying of Aids,
there is the light of God;
in every human person, no matter how broken, sinful,
hardened, dominating or cruel,
there is a spring of water waiting to flow forth.

If you walk with Jesus along this path,
he will lead you
to the poor, the weak, the lonely and the oppressed,
not with fear and despair,
not with feelings of guilt and helplessness,
not with anger and revolt,
not with theories and preconceived solutions,
but with a new and deeper
peace and love and hope.

And he will reveal to you the new meaning
of pain and darkness;
how joy springs
from the wounds of brokenness.
He will reveal to you

2

that he is hidden in
the poor, the weak, the lonely and the oppressed.

He will reveal to you the way to refind,
rebuild, renew and receive
the relationship of gentle love and fidelity
that is at the origin of all existence.
It will be revealed as a tiny seed
but one from which can grow new life for the world.

Let us walk together along this path
with our sisters and brothers
in this broken world of ours.
Let us walk together along this path
with Jesus,
and discover that it is a path of hope.

Part I
Our Broken Body

We are no longer in a world filled with optimism.
That was the world of the 'fifties and 'sixties.
The terrible war with Nazi Germany had ended.
People were weary and wanted to build peace;
countries long-dominated by colonialism
were being liberated;
economic expansion seemed to promise the possibility of a
                              good life to be had by all!
There were high hopes that
poverty and hunger would be banished from the earth,
and that each human person would find freedom from want
and freedom to create their own destiny.

But in that terrible war,
two fearful seeds were sown:
the mushroom cloud over Hiroshima and Nagasaki,
which killed hundreds of thousands of people
in one fateful instant
and maimed so many others;
and the camps
in Auschwitz, Dachau, Ravensbruck, Buchenwald, Belsen –
places of extermination of the Jewish people;
some six million bodies burnt in ovens,
a cruelty and a horror that few could believe.
These seeds are still with us.

Now we are approaching the year 2000 –
optimism has given way to hopelessness
and illusions are fading.
We are confronted with the stark reality
of a broken humanity.

4

We are no longer isolated in small villages,
ignorant of what is going on in the rest of the world.
Our television sets show us the hunger of Ethiopia,
        the earthquake in Mexico,
        the refugee camps in Cambodia,
        the war in Lebanon,
        the cry and the anger of the Palestinian people,
        the crushing of Solidarity in Poland,
        the agony of South Africa.
We can see the pain of our world
as we watch the news,
drinking our beer in the comfort of our sitting room,
with the security of doors locked against any intrusion.

There seems to be nothing we can do to help.
We just look at the horror
and hear the cry of the poor.
We feel helpless and guilty
because there is nothing we can do,
and we ourselves are caught up in our own need
for comfort and security.

Television can show us other pictures:
flashing, changing, thrilling, colourful pictures,
pictures that are seductive,
exciting wild, passionate emotions.
But they are only pictures on a screen.
As we look at them, we cannot be really present to people
as one person to another,
sharing or listening to one another.
For there is no relationship, compassion or communion –
they are only pictures that tend to isolate us even more
in a world of dreams.

If there is a person in pain in our village
or a house that has burnt down,
or if there is some other local catastrophe,
perhaps we can do something about it.

5

But what can we do about the things we see on television
happening in the Sahel or in Central America?
What can *we* do to repair the broken body of humanity?

Wars drag on endlessly,
people continue to starve.
Everywhere there are terrible inequalities.
Workers are exploited,
refugees are fleeing in terror.
Peoples are oppressed,
while politicians engage in petty squabbling
and churches fight with one another.
Today, as we approach the year 2000 there appears to be
                                                    so little hope.

So perhaps the only thing to do
is to hide in front of our television sets;
and forget the pain of this broken world,
the pain of a broken humanity,
about which we can do nothing.
Let us change the channel when the pictures are too ghastly
and look for other stations,
a tantalizing film,
some other light amusement –
any form of distraction.

For the first time in history,
children in a small, traditional village in Egypt or India
are able to watch films made in America.
They are influenced by values
completely foreign to the values inculcated by their parents.
The intimacy of the home is violated
and the experience of cultural stability is destroyed
at an age too early for a child to assimilate.
The result is deep confusion
and the breakdown of family relationships.
Children grow up in a world of dreams and illusion
manipulated from elsewhere,

6

exciting insatiable desires,
creating false needs,
and turning people in upon themselves,
unable to think for themselves
or to take responsibility.

The terrible spectre of the mushroom cloud,
of the nuclear bomb,
looms over humanity –
this folly of mankind,
driven in a race for superiority in weapons and warfare.
All the money and human resources being poured
into the manufacture of bombs,
the making of new, more destructive weapons,
weapons that will operate more quickly, more precisely,
more powerfully, more totally –
while many women in Africa still spend hours each day
just bringing water to their homes!

Never before has the cry for peace been so great.
Never before has the danger been so immense.
Today our earth, our beautiful earth,
could be totally shattered,
ruined by these weapons.
Today conflict is too dangerous,
for all life could be destroyed.
With all the vast sophistication in our weaponry
we are at the mercy
of a momentary error
in human judgement or technical functioning.
We know that and are filled with fear.

Yet everywhere armed conflict *is* rampant:
terrorism of all sorts is increasing.
People are imprisoned, tortured or disappear.
Dictatorships, whether marxist or military,

are crushing people,
preventing them from speaking,
taking from them their human rights.
And there is the weak and painful cry
of the unborn child aborted
or of the unwelcome child with disabilities.

And, more and more, those who were crushed or put aside
are rising up in anger and frustration,
in armed revolt
to claim their place, their land, their right to live.

Is violence the only solution?
Is there any other way?
For violence always engenders violence.
How often the ideals of liberation
are swallowed up in
more terrible violence,
more total oppression!

Can there be another way to peace?

In richer countries life is dominated
by constant competition,
by the struggle for success and power.
In Canada I saw a sign in a classroom:
'It is a crime not to excel.'
Each one of us must succeed;
if we do not, we will have no status in society,
no work, no home.
We must win the prize or else be discarded.
So we learn to harden our hearts and fight and struggle
to be first,
to be better than anyone else.

Those who cannot make it fall by the wayside,
in sadness and anger.

They will quickly be lost in the world of drugs
or be drawn, confused and bewildered,
into gangs with their own hierarchies
and values of success.
Others fall into a pit of despair,
knowing there is no place, no work, no future for them,
maybe lured into suicide.

Never before have we been so aware of the immense gap
between those who have and those who have not.
The poor are mainly in the southern hemisphere
where the population is growing;
but they are also in the slums of every city,
out of work.
Others are locked up in institutions and hospitals.
The rich get richer,
holding onto their power, their prestige and their privileges,
increasingly afraid and disturbed by the poor,
frightened of facing a reality
which calls for change.

The terribly broken body of humanity
separated by walls of fear;
people closed in on themselves,
fearful of differences,
seeking only security.

Never before have families been so broken:
men and women are compelled to work,
not to find personal fulfilment
or to create beauty and harmony,
but to pay the debts for the car, the house,
and for all the things
advertisements tell them they cannot live without!
Fatigue, exhaustion, stress and aggression
accompany the long hours of travel to and from work.

Families are displaced and uprooted
as they try to find work
or a job with more money,
but the real loss is in the quality of relationship:
men and women unable to meet each other's needs,
expecting too much from one another.
The cry of loneliness and the need for love
can so quickly evoke hatred or a sense of imprisonment;
tenderness turns into aggression,
leading to separation and divorce.
Is it possible to love,
to be faithful in love?
Or do we exist in a chaotic world
where love is only a myth?
Is love anything more
than just seeking to fill up one's own emptiness,
using the other for one's own pleasure and power?
The experience of separation is so painful,
looking back on the ecstasy of love
as nothing but a dream or an illusion.

So many of us in our world today have walked this path
of broken relationships.
It is so painful to discover inner emptiness,
the inability to love,
the experience of sexuality which is no longer gift of self
in a covenant relationship,
but rather self-seeking pleasure
turned in upon self.

That is why our big cities
have become places of loneliness.
It is terrible to feel so alone
in a crowd.
People everywhere,
surging around,
but feeling all alone.
Who will love me tonight?

Maybe a chance meeting?
And maybe I will die like so many others
in the void of this loneliness.

A child is hurt
when it senses its father and mother are too tired
    or too angry, too empty or too busy
    to welcome it,
    to play with it
    with laughter, relaxation and joy.
The little child suffers so much
from the discord between parents.
Its tender heart is too vulnerable and fragile;
it needs security, protection,
a creative love flowing from unity.
When it senses unhappiness and conflict
the child is plunged into insecurity,
feeling a terrible fear and loneliness,
a despair that overwhelms the body.

Many people today
are the fruit of the broken body of their family:
children are insecure and vulnerable,
lacking roots,
unable to grow peacefully,
to know their own minds,
or hear the inner wisdom of their own hearts.
Today we are seeing
the birth of a newly fragile humanity:
lonely, bewildered,
lacking references and a sense of belonging;
feeling empty,
but finding nothing to fill the emptiness.

Much of my life over the last twenty years
has been with men and women having a mental handicap.
I have seen and touched their pain:
the terrible pain of being a disappointment to their parents.
They feel weak, unable to cope with life
which moves so fast around them.
This feeling of not being wanted, just as they are,
engenders a sense of guilt.
They feel they have hurt their parents,
because they were not a cause of joy
but rather a source of worry and pain.
So they think they are worthless, just a nuisance –
maybe even evil.
And from this loneliness arises anguish and confusion,
an inner brokenness,
no trust in themselves or in others.
This in turn leads to violence,
depression, disturbed behaviour,
and so they are put aside even more,
rejected.
They sense that they belong nowhere and to no one.

The pain of those who cannot fit
into the mainstream of society is so great!
They feel useless, a dead weight.
This feeling is shared by many old people,
or by people out of work,
        immigrants,
        fragile and weak people,
        people with disabilities or chronic sickness –
        whether physical or mental –
        people caught up in obsessions
        of eating, alcohol or drugs.

It seems better to escape
into a world of dreams and illusion or even madness
rather than live in this pain of isolation and despair.
The dream world is sometimes so much better

than the real world:
There one feels at least a sense of control,
a measure of consolation.

But many people who appear powerful and successful
can also feel worthless deep inside themselves.
They have money, power, education, status,
but they lack what is essential:
a heart that is free and loving,
a knowledge that they are loved.
They seem unable to relate,
and feel broken and empty inside;
they sense that they are wanted
only by those who seek money and power.
They too feel they belong to no one.
They feel that terrible pain of being unable to love,
of isolation,
unable to break out of their shell
to relate with trust and faithfulness,
in communion with others.

Those who are fearful of relationships
often hide in dreams or theories
or escape into distractions of all kinds
or into projects that keep them busy.
They avoid people
who might be aggressive or challenge them.
They maintain contact only with those who flatter them
and are members of the same club.

So many today feel inadequate in their capacity to relate,
            to love,
            to listen deeply,
            to be compassionate.
In some ways they are cut off
from the deep feelings of their hearts
and their emotions.
They are afraid of relationships,

because these awaken emotions they do not understand
and arouse energies
over which they feel they have no control.
It is safer to live by cold reason.

There is a great danger today of killing the heart,
of living in this cold world of reason,
where people are no longer people
but objects to be studied and organized
by rational intellect.
The world of technology can stifle what is human.
Genetic engineering
means choosing the baby of dreams and calculations,
rather than receiving the child as a gift
born of love.
And so today
man and woman are in danger
of being programmed like computers.
They are no longer seen as people
with hearts capable of love and gift of self.

The pain of our world is so great.
Which way do we turn?
Is there any real hope?
Can there be any response to the terrible cries around us
    and within us?

Today some feel that the only answer
is national security:
defending themselves more effectively,
clarifying their identity more sharply,
getting rid of strangers
and all who disturb.
Any form of pluralism in this vision becomes dangerous
because it may bring confusion and erode identity.
So new barriers are built,

developing a sense of being the strongest,
of being the best.

In such a world,
the Christian churches seem to many people irrelevant,
for they too are more a cause of division and of war
than a source of unity and peace.
To walk down the street and see
    the Baptist church,
    the Lutheran church,
    the Anglican church,
    the Presbyterian church,
    the Methodist church,
    the Roman Catholic church,
    this or that church,
    each one preaching its own Jesus,
        collecting money,
        building more buildings
        defending its own frontiers.
All this seems unbearable, intolerable hypocrisy!
Where *is* our hope?
Where are the prophets of peace today?

Maybe these words seem pessimistic.
Truly, there are signs of hope in our world today;
people are rising up, believing in life, in human life,
yearning to be peacemakers,
struggling for unity.
But many do not see these signs.
They only see a broken world:
    a world of war and despair,
    a world governed by fear,
    a world of pain and suffering,
    a chaotic world of greed and oppression,
        of lust for power, for pleasure and for security.
They feel despondent and without hope,
but somewhere in them there is a longing
to discover the road to peace.

15

Those who are weak are so frequently crushed.
Weakness is despised, laughed at, rejected.
At the same time it is easy
to fool, manipulate and use weak people.
It is the story, the terrible story of slavery.
But it is also the story of people with disabilities,
or people struck down with sickness.

It seems that many people crush the weak
because they themselves, somewhere in their lives,
were crushed.
People who have experienced injustice,
perhaps in the forgotten depths of childhood,
often take a secret revenge on weaker people,
on those who cannot answer back.
The weak and the poor are often the scapegoats –
nobody defends them,
and they are forced to accept the violence
of other human beings.

But over the years of living with people
who have been crushed or put aside
I have discovered something new.
They have led me gently
into the depths of my own heart
filled, as it is, with light and darkness.
They have led me into the mystery of Jesus
and of his message,
and into the secret of humanity and of its history.
They have shown me the light shining in the darkness.
They have begun to reveal to me with greater clarity
God's unfolding plan for humanity –
a plan that prophets and saints have announced for years,
but our ears are deaf.

Let me tell you about this plan
and the beginning of it all.

Part II
God's Unfolding Plan

Being Created in Wholeness

Our God is a God of life and light.
When God creates, it is life and light that is given.
To understand the depth of our brokenness
we need to look at the wholeness in which we were created,
a wholeness that comes from total communion with God.

On one of the doorways of the Cathedral of Chartres
there is a statue of God creating Adam.
It is a beautiful statue.
The Father is symbolized through the body of Christ.
He has the face of Christ.
Adam has the same face,
though younger and without a beard.

This statue radiates a deep serenity and silence.
God is gently drawing Adam out of the mud.
Adam is resting on the breast of God
as John rested on the breast of Jesus.
They are both smiling, filled with a profound joy;
as if God the artist was saying, 'You are beautiful',
and Adam was saying, 'You are beautiful'.
They are in communion with one another.

As human artists,
we can create beautiful statues, paintings, poems and books,
we can compose and play magnificent music.
We can experience their beauty
we can see how they open us to eternal truths.

17

But none of these works of ours can look at us and say,
'I love you – you are beautiful.'

The work of the hands of God is a living person,
a human heart.
And this human person can look at God and say,
'I love you; you are beautiful.'
This human person can freely enter
into relationship with God.
They can speak together.
They can rest in one another.
They can celebrate together.
The maker and the made can be in love with one another.
Only God, the source of all life,
can take this great risk of creation
– for the 'made' can say 'yes', but also 'no'.

The statue at Chartres
does not depict the creation of woman.
But God did not want man to be alone,
so God created woman, alike, yet different.
Man could not see and touch God,
though he could hear God in the secret of his being.
But God wanted man to express his love,
not to remain buried in himself or lost in work.
So God created woman.

Man could look at woman
and see in her eyes the light of God.
Woman could look at man
and see in his eyes the light of God.
They could speak to each other and say,
'You are beautiful, I love you.'
They could kiss each other with tender love,
they could contemplate each other
in the naked beauty of their bodies
and give thanks for all of creation.

In this union with one another, they were whole.
Together they formed one body.
To be one body is to be covenanted together,
each in need of the other,
each having a special gift to offer the other,
complementing the other.
They need each other to give life.
Alone man or woman can use wood to build a house;
alone each one can produce *things*.
But to create life,
man and woman must unite physically and in love.

Only God, the artist of life,
can make an object that is living,
with whom it is possible to enter into dialogue.
Yet through procreation, God gives to man and woman
the power to transmit life.
But in doing so they act, not as artists,
but as humble instruments of nature.
The child that will be born is of their flesh;
they will be able to enter into relationship with the child,
but they cannot create a child of their dreams.
They can only receive the child that is given to them.

Adam loved Eve; Eve loved Adam.
They were one body, one love, one spirit.
Each one could give to the other,
each one could drink from the other.
Gentle communion,
gentle passion flowing one from another.
And this communion rose up as incense to God.
Their love, their gift of self to each other, their unity,
was a celebration, a thanksgiving, a praise.
God rejoiced to see their wholeness
and their joy in one another,
reflecting the glory of the divine.
And it was from the depth of their communion with God
and with each other

that they were destined to give birth to children,
and grow as a family,
develop the earth with all its potential
and consecrate it to God.

But the harmony and communion between Adam and Eve,
and with all creation broke.
For the harmony was linked
to communion with their Creator.
It was like water flowing from a source,
filling up two ponds,
which in turn overflowed into a stream.
If the source is blocked,
the ponds will be empty and the stream will dry up.
If the energy of love is stopped,
then it cannot flow from one human heart to another.

At a particular moment
Adam and Eve said 'no' to God.
They turned away,
blocking off this energy of love.
They refused to be dependent upon the energy
flowing from God.
They were seduced by the Evil One
who had said,
    you can do it alone,
    you can be like God,
    you can be free,
    you don't have to obey and be like children,
    you can be adults.
They turned away and closed themselves up
from the source of life.
And then they discovered they were empty,
naked, alone, and in despair.

It is this severing act which is the source
of all our experience of inner conflict.
There are a thousand ways

by which we try to avoid this reality,
ways in which we try to plaster over the cracks,
to hold things together by force or law or culture,
or by filling ourselves up
with projects and passing pleasures.

Man and woman are in danger of looking to each other
to fill up that emptiness.
But when cut off from the source
of the infinite energy of God's love
they fail,
and then become frustrated
because their expectations and needs are not met
or because each demands from the other
what, humanly speaking, is impossible and unreasonable.

When communion with God is broken,
full communion with each other is impossible.
They cannot give water,
    since the well at the source of their being is not flowing.
They cannot give life,
    for something has died within them.
Man will tend to dominate woman
and woman to find compensation in the children.
Their bodies may still function
in a way that symbolizes wholeness.
They can copulate and conceive a child,
but the essence of wholeness and communion
is lost.
The harmony
between their hearts, their heads and their sexuality
is gone.
The pain of this loss is so deeply buried;
often it is not recognized.

The yearning for, the memory of,
the original wholeness and communion
may at times come alive, in all of us.

Holy men and women of all ages and places
have lived in this knowledge,
have reminded us of this truth
which lies beyond our experience of brokenness.

Yet brokenness is pervasive,
it takes on a life of its own
and becomes an opportunity for the Evil One
to exercise his powers.

And to the extent that this is so,
man will be unable to enter truly into
communion with woman.
He can desire woman, he can use her as a servant,
as a bearer of his children, or as an object of his desire,
instead of a person to be loved freely.
His contemplation of her naked body
will be marred by the memory of a lost dream
sought again through self-centred pleasure
which can become a greed, even a compulsion,
destroying the capacity for gentle communion
and gift of self.

And so it is with woman:
she may submissively accept her husband's attitude,
and the culture which assumes
she cannot grow to full freedom as a person.
She will cry out to be touched,
more out of her hunger and need,
than out of the desire to give herself.

Nakedness exposes the reality of emptiness,
anguish, loneliness,
and the feeling of death.
And out of this experience
comes both a closing in, a fleeing from reality,
        fleeing the pain of the other,
        a need to cover up, hide away,

and also a lashing out in anger,
a desire to hurt and destroy the other.

If communion between man and woman is lost,
relationship with their children is inevitably affected.
It may become impossible for parents to love their children
with a freedom-giving love.
They become possessive,
making the children feel guilty
if they do not conform to parental desires.

Possessive love is stifling –
children cannot grow,
life cannot flow.
   And naturally there will be anger.
   A child is afraid of this anger,
   experienced as it is in cosmic proportions.
   Children must push this anger down,
   for it is too dangerous,
   too unbearable, to live with.
And so on the surface
they smile, and say 'yes',
but deep down this terrible anger lies hidden,
coupled with a guilt beyond endurance.

The spiral of violence deepens.
When communion is broken
the consequences multiply and spread.
Children may begin to direct their anger
to brothers and sisters.

True indeed it is that the sin of brokenness
is visited upon us from generation to generation.
From this original broken state
it is impossible to love freely;
from the lack of being loved freely and with respect
stems more anger and frustration;
this creates guilt and cannot be expressed.

So the seeds of hate, of rivalry,
and maybe depression, are watered.

And the other side of anger and hatred
is fear.
And because of fear
the body of humanity began to fragment,
ethnic groups formed,
each governed by rigid laws, traditions and customs,
trying to maintain the strict unity
felt necessary to survive
against all the powers of death and destruction.
This is the tragic story of humanity
as we read it.

Within each group
caste systems and hierarchies were adopted.
The roles of man and woman were defined.
The place and duties of slave and serf and manual worker
were strictly determined,
while the privileges of lords and princes
and all those who had material or priestly power
were protected.

In such rigid unity
the gifts of the individual person could so easily be stifled:
everyone had to conform to the group,
because this gave security.
Personal reflective growth was restricted
in the name of obedience to authority and the laws it upheld.

In such a system
those who transgressed the laws and the customs
sinned against the group.
They were considered destructive of the good of the whole,
and had to be banished,
preferably pushed into outer darkness.

But so it is in many places and countries today
with all the weak and 'useless' ones,
those suffering from mental or physical handicaps,
men and women who are sick and lame and blind,
or suffering from leprosy –
those whose very existence in some way
transgresses the laws and the customs.
They become outcasts,
pushed into the lanes and byways to beg –
if they are allowed to survive at all.
They are so deep a threat
to the artificial security of rigidity,
awakening memories of the fear and helplessness
that have been pushed down
into hidden areas of the unconscious,
feelings to be forgotten or denied at all costs.

People sometimes believe
that those who threaten the cohesion of the group
must be possessed by evil spirits;
often they are branded as mad.
In almost all societies, whether primitive or sophisticated,
whether of the past or the present,
this process of enforcing conformity,
by rejecting any deviation,
has been a normal pattern.

Only occasionally have some societies recognized
that those who are 'abnormal' are in some ways prophetic,
pointing to a world of truth
which transcends their experience of normality.

The Plan Unfolds

God's plan for humanity
began like a tiny seed.

In this seed
is contained the magnificence of a huge cedar tree,
and within this tiny seed
lies the future of millions of other seeds
which will take form as the tree grows.

  In the seed is life,
  and all is marvellously programmed within.
  As the seed unfolds,
  as the child is conceived,
  so it begins to grow
  and we begin to see its beauty.
  All that was hidden in the seed
  begins to be revealed
  as it unfolds.

The fullness of the plan of God
  is an unfathomable secret,
  known in its entirety only to God.
But each person
in the long, immensely long, line of generations
is able to say 'yes' or 'no' freely
to the unfolding of this plan –
a very little 'yes' or 'no' –
but freely said.

To the poverty of our human minds
the possibility of a destiny conceived by God,
and freedom,
seem contradictory.
Yet it is not so.
For the wisdom of God
and his respect for each person is so great,
that a destiny of ultimate fulfilment,
and individual freedom,
are gently married,
  and the glory of God and of creation
  flows from this union.

26

God has the secret
of loving us to freedom,
inviting us to share in the creativity of love.

Because so many of us have experienced
a love coming from parents – or others –
that is stifling or crippling or possessive,
it is difficult to believe we are loved
by a love that brings us to freedom,
and that God's plan goes far beyond
the wonder and beauty of the creation we know.

For though the communion between man and woman
and their God was broken,
all was not lost.

We can still see,
in the glorious harmony of creation,
the body of God,
the visible revealing the invisible hand and heart and mind
of the Creator.

The harmony which reigns in the universe
reflects the wisdom and majesty
of the divine being.
        The sun and the moon,
        the immensity of the stars and galaxies
        measured in millions of light years,
        the ordered movement of planets,
        vast harmonies of energies.

        And our earth,
        the beautiful warm earth,
        receiving water from the clouds.
        And water
        springing and bubbling forth from the earth,
        water of the seas,

27

water bringing life,
to the garden, a wonderful garden
with myriads of trees and flowers and fruits,
birds singing,
animals of all kinds,
tiny insects;
all are marvellously linked together,
married in one whole body.
Our earth brings forth food and wine
to nourish what is most beautiful in creation,
man and woman,
given to each other
to celebrate this oneness of body.
Their unity
becomes a dance upon the earth;
their intimate communion
becomes a song of praise and love,
mounting towards God
like incense
gathered into the unity of the Trinity.

And all this life
from within
brings forth new life;
flowers and animals
birds and fishes
intertwined,
giving life
from generation to generation,
male and female
in love with each other,
bearing fruit,
much fruit –
the incredible creativity of God.

Yes, the deepest song of everything in creation
reflects the unity of the Trinity:
three persons poured out in love for one another.

Great scientists of today,
standing on the shoulders of great scientists of the past,
have hardly begun to unravel the secret
of our universe;
our insights into the secrets of nature, of light and life,
give us but a glimpse
into the incredibly creative, wonderful intelligence
and glory of God,
and how intricately interwoven
are all the processes of life.

Sub-atomic physicists are discovering
that the tiniest particles,
separated by thousands of miles,
respond to each other,
are in relationship.

Ecologists are discovering
that nature is so deeply inter-related,
that the tiniest insect has its significance for the whole,
that there can be immense repercussions
if just one species is destroyed or depleted.

Yet it is true that today
our earth is marked
by human beings fighting each other,
and polluting and exploiting nature.
We have hurt each other
and the garden
that has been given for our nourishment and our delight.
Most of us are out of touch with each other
and with the earth of our own bodies,
preoccupied with production and security and comfort,
preparing armaments,
building frontiers.
What a discrepancy between
the joyful winging of birds
and the fear in men and women,

between the freedom of dolphins playing in the sea
and men and women becoming slaves
to comfort and pleasure.

Yet God had a marvellous plan
to reveal the love that burns within the Trinity,
and to bring men and women
to an even fuller unity and glory

At the centre of that plan
is God's desire to become flesh,
    to take on our human condition,
    to put on human nature,
    so that our Creator
    would be touched and heard and loved,
    so that our brokenness
    could be healed into a new wholeness,
    so that we could become again one perfect body.

And the fulfilling of this plan
involved a woman
who would mother the Word made flesh,
a mother who would be the sign of the Eternal Father
and in whose human womb,
created from the bowels of the earth,
the Word would become flesh.

He would become the new Adam
rejoicing in the new Eve –
Jesus,
rejoicing in the woman Mary.
And they would lead a multitude
into the knowledge of the Father,
into the heart of the Trinity aflame in ecstasy,
into the wedding feast.

God would repair the brutal damage
of the first Adam and the first Eve

as they turned away from communion,
wanting authority and power,
refusing dependence upon their source.
The plan of God
is to heal and repair the damaged body,
to bring it to a new and fuller beauty,
to a new and deeper fecundity.

Our human nature is so skilfully made
by the unseen hand of God
that even within our brokenness
lies the seed that will lead us back to wholeness.
The very fear that inhabits us
draws men and women together.
True this togetherness no longer stems
from a unity of love and of personal freedom,
but is prompted by the need
for collective security against the powers of death.

From the emptiness of Adam and Eve
rises up a cry, a craving, a thirst
to be filled.
It is man and woman's incessant search to be filled
that pushes them forward into the unknown.
But the personal anguish is too great,
the breaking point at the heart of our humanity
is too painful.
In itself, it is literally unbearable and cannot be faced
without the knowledge which transcends it,
without the love which redeems it.

Only Jesus, because he is the Word in whom we are created,
could go to that point of ultimate emptiness, separation,
the broken communion with God.

God watched over humanity
as it grew over the earth.

Through history and evolution
God was preparing the future.
In times of great darkness and pain,
or when the forces of destruction intensified,
holy men and women,
prophets and philosophers of truth,
rose up.
Frequently they were healers of the spirit and the body,
men and women of wisdom
calling the people to righteous living.
Their knowledge of God
often came to them through dreams and visions;
and at particular times in history
they revealed certain aspects of the universal way to holiness.
This way became embodied in specific laws and traditions
and so humanity evolved.

But there were also false prophets inspired by evil spirits
who tried to undo the work of unity and holiness.
The walls of fear separating ethnic groups
rose higher and stronger.
Within the group there was a strict unity
and a code of behaviour accepted by all,
but this only accentuated the differences
between the groups –
differences which fostered feelings of contempt
and hostility.
The body of each group had a certain solidity
but it could not be whole
because the inner freedom of the individual person
was suppressed or, if that was not possible,
the person was cast out from the group.
So the body of all humanity
became more and more broken and fragmented
as different languages and customs,
different philosophies and religions, developed.
One group, feeling better, wiser and holier than the others,
tried to overpower another,

sometimes through war,
and through genocide,
sometimes through more subtle oppression
such as social or economic exploitation.
Anger and hatred continued to smoulder,
exploding from time to time.
Empires grew up
seeking to dominate and enslave the world,
sometimes doing so
in the name of repairing the broken body of humanity,
promising to bring peace through force.

It was in and through one of these peoples
that God chose to become flesh,
to become one of us,
to be touched and heard and seen and loved,
and even hated.
It was necessary to enter into this small part of our world
in order to draw
the whole body of humanity into its true oneness.
Only a body
that could contain the experience of all humankind
could reconcile heaven and earth.
A Word that did not become flesh,
however true or holy,
would have no power to endure.

So God chose Abraham,
and promised him descendants
as numerous as the stars of the sky.
In her old age, Sarah, his wife, gave birth to Isaac.
Isaac and Rebecca gave birth to Jacob,
and thus was born the Jewish people.

But Abraham, through Hagar his servant,
had another son, Ishmael.
The angel of the Lord said to Hagar:

'I will multiply your descendants in such a way
that none will be able to count them.'
Thus was born the Arab peoples,
and they too had a destiny
in God's plan.

God watched over the Jewish people
throughout the centuries of their fidelity and infidelities.
He sent prophets,
Moses, Isaiah, Jeremiah, Ezekiel
and many others to sustain hope
and faithfulness in the people,
reminding them of the love
through which they were born and held and protected.
And God announced that from this people
a Saviour, a Messiah,
the Anointed One,
the Holy One, would be born.

So, when the time was ripe,
God chose a young Jewish woman,
Mary, espoused to Joseph,
and revealed through the message of an angel
that she would become the mother of Christ:
      'Hail,
      O favoured one,
      the Lord is with thee.
      Do not be afraid, Mary,
      for your have found favour with God.
      You shall conceive in your womb
      and bear a son.
      And you shall name him Jesus.
      He shall be great and will be called
      Son of the Most High.
      The Lord God will give him the throne
      of David his father
      and his reign will never end.
      The Holy Spirit will come upon you,

and the power of the most High
will cover you with his shadow.
That is why the child to be born
will be called
Holy,
Son of God.'

And the name of Jesus means
        God saves,
        God heals,
        God makes whole.

Jesus

The Word became flesh
and his name is *Jesus*.
He came as a tiny child
in the womb of a woman.
He was clothed in the vulnerability of a child
in need of its mother,
crying out for protection and help.
The love of a mother
is the only real security an infant has;
without it, the life of the child is in danger
of being overwhelmed
by a terrible fear
a fear of death,
which will block development of the emotions,
the mind and the spirit.
The Almighty became a helpless child
utterly dependent on a relationship with a woman,
a relationship of love.

At birth
Jesus had no security but the arms of Mary
and the presence of Joseph.

He became a child refugee
as the family fled into Egypt,
encountering dangers and uncertainties.
And after their return
they settled in the village of Nazareth, in Galilee:
a village of poor people, looked down upon by others,
inhabiting caves in the hillside.
And there Jesus lived in simplicity for thirty years.
He worked with his hands,
being a son of the carpenter, Joseph.
We know nothing of those years
except that he did not make himself known.
The Word made flesh
lived the humble, lowly life of a poor family.
He lived the beatitudes before announcing them.

Then for three short years he preached.
He came to announce good news to the poor,
sight to the blind,
and liberty to prisoners and to the oppressed.
This was the mission he proclaimed
at the beginning of his public ministry,
when he left the poor village of Nazareth.
He left his mother,
and his work,
to give this message.

His teaching is simple,
contained in what he called
the new commandment:
'Love one another as I have loved you.'
Love your enemies.
Love those who hate and persecute you.
Love those who have become outcast
and those who are excluded from the group
because they are 'useless', non-productive:
the blind, the lame, the sick,
the poor and the lepers.

Love not just those of your own tribe,
your own class, family or people,
but those who are different,
those who are strangers,
who are strange to your ways,
who come from different cultural and religious traditions,
who seem odd,
those you do not understand.
Love as the Samaritan loved the man he found
      beaten up by robbers,
            somewhere on the road between Jerusalem and Jericho.

To love is to open our hearts to people
      to listen to them,
      to appreciate them
            and see in them their own unique value,
      to wish deeply that they may live and grow.
To love is to give our lives for one another.
It is to forgive,
and to be compassionate.

But by ourselves we cannot love in this way.
Jesus came to take away the dynamics of fear
that close us in upon ourselves
as we try to cover up our vulnerability and inner loneliness.
He only asks that we follow him,
opening our hearts to him
in a personal relationship,
trusting
and believing in him,
– as the One sent by the Father
to give us this love
which flows from the heart of the Father;
– as the One sent by the Father
to make us children of the Father,
beloved children,
called to enter into the glory and love of the Trinity;

– as the One sent by the Father
to take away the sins and the violence of the world
and all forms of fear and guilt;
– as the One through whose body
our bodies become whole;
– as the One who will fill us with his Spirit
if we accept to die to a spirit of greed, rivalry and selfishness.

Jesus teaches us how to live
giving us the charter of the beatitudes:
Blessed are the poor in spirit,
the meek and humble,
those who weep and mourn,
those who hunger and thirst for God's ways,
the merciful,
the pure of heart,
the peace-makers,
those who are persecuted.

He tells us not to want the first place in every gathering,
not to seek power,
even if it is to do good,
but to seek the last place,
to be humble and close to the poor,
and those who are broken or in pain.
For it is in them that we shall discover
the secret and the source of love.
He tells us too
that if we want to enter the Kingdom of God,
we must become like little children.
There is no other way,
for the secrets of the Kingdom are hidden
from the powerful, the prudent and the clever
closed up in self-satisfaction,
and are revealed to little ones.

Jesus is no ordinary prophet or holy man.
He did not come only

to teach us the right way to live
so that there would be peace in our hearts
and upon this earth.
He did not come just to give a message of hope
and encourage us to follow his teachings.
No, he is more than a prophet and a teacher:
In reality he *is* the message.
It is his person, his love, and his heart
that are the message.
Certainly his words are important –
but more important still is his person, his body.
It was his body, not just his mind,
that radiated the perfection of divine energy.
It was his body
that became the perfect channel of transformation:
total receptivity to the power and love of the Father.

That is why he cried out in the temple
    'If any one thirsts let him come to me to drink!'
    'Come to me all you who are laden
    and heavy-burdened
    and I will give you rest.'
    'He who eats my body and drinks my blood
    has eternal life
    and I will raise him up on the last day.'
    'He who sees me, sees the Father,
    for the Father and I are one.'
    'Anyone who remains in me will bear much fruit.'
    'He who believes in me will live forever.'

Jesus is not just one who shows the way,
who announces the truth,
who inspires people as other prophets have done.
He *is* the Way, the Truth and the Life.
He *is* the Light of the World,
He *is* the Resurrection.
He *is* the vine and we are the branches.
He *is* Love.

He *is* the new temple in whom resides the Divinity,
His body is this temple, to whom all will come,
    to rest and to drink,
    to find life and forgiveness.
He is the Saviour who comes,
not to judge or condemn our sin,
but to free us from the yoke of guilt,
    that terribly heavy guilt,
and to free us from fear –
    the fear of death
        of evil spirits,
        of rejection and abandonment,
        of doing wrong,
        of being wrong,
        of total emptiness;
    the fear which makes us clutch on to the false security
        of the group,
        refusing to become our own true selves
        in the image of our God

He comes to make us children of the Father,
revealing the Father's incredible tenderness and hope
    for each one of us.
He comes to heal our wounded hearts
by entering into a relationship of love
    with each one of us.
Then through this relationship of love,
    this communion,
he teaches us to open up in a relationship of love
    with other people.

As I read the story of Jesus,
the simple facts of his life,
I am touched most by his freedom, his truthfulness,

his compassion and his special love for the poor,
the sinner and the rejected.

Jesus is freedom

Yes, he is a free man,
one might say, scandalously free:
he was not blocked or enslaved by his own culture,
by the ways of the Jewish people.
He had no need to seek popularity or votes.
There is no fear in him of what people might think.
He speaks vehemently to the pharisees and the scribes,
calling them hypocrites, a brood of vipers,
comparing them to whited sepulchres,
which outwardly appear beautiful
but inside are full of dead bones and all kinds of corruption.

He speaks sternly to the rich:
    'Woe unto you the rich;
    woe unto you who are filled now;
    woe unto you who laugh now;
    woe unto you when everyone speaks well of you.'
    'It is harder for a rich person to enter the Kingdom
    than for a camel to pass through the eye of a needle.'

Freely he speaks to the despised Samaritan woman
and asks her for water,
Freely he lets the woman, a victim of prostitution,
    wash his feet with her tears
    and dry them with her hair,
    unconcerned that people are scandalized.
Freely he mixes with sinners and publicans,
    who could not enter the temple
    and were locked into their guilt.
Freely he heals on the sabbath day,
    undeterred by the fury of the pharisees.
Freely he hears the call of the Roman centurion, the enemy,
    and answers his cry with love.

Freely he invites himself into the house of Zaccheus,
    the rich but rejected publican,
    ignoring the murmurings of the righteous.
Freely he touches the lepers
    and mixes with the outcasts of society,
    the uncouth rabble.
Freely he announces that his body is real food,
    his blood real drink,
    even though he knows people will turn away,
    unable to follow him any further.
Yes, Jesus is an incredibly free man
who cannot be pinned down, labelled or put in a box.
He confines himself to no specific group,
whether political or social,
national or religious.
He is free to do the work of his Father
and to announce to every person,
whoever he or she may be,
that he loves them
and that they in turn can become lovers of every person
universal brothers and sisters.
He is free with the freedom of God.

Jesus is truth

He cannot bear hypocrisy or duplicity.
He cannot tolerate the fact
that those who proclaim the laws of God
are the ones who crush the weak and the helpless.
He struggles against the Father of Lies,
    the Prince of this world,
    who tries to keep people in confusion,
    division and darkness.
He speaks with authority,
    not like the pharisees and the scribes,
    who taught by giving the opinions of different masters
    (always a safe way of teaching!).
He claims the truth and announces it freely:

'Verily, I say unto you.'
He accepts the consequences of that truth
and the aggression and hatred it provokes in others,
because the truth is uncomfortable
and people would rather have confusion.

Jesus is compassion

It is as though he is attracted in a special way,
almost like a magnet,
to those who are suffering, or broken or rejected.
He knows human weakness and poverty,
and he knows that the separation of death is unbearable.

No barriers were built
around the heart of Jesus
to protect his vulnerability;
his heart is continually open and loving,
yearning to enter into the to-and-fro
of friendship, relationship, love and trust,
and to be filled by people.
Thus he remains so vulnerable to rejection.
His heart is a heart that suffers terribly.
It is always so close to anguish and agony,
and to the tears of loneliness.
Jesus knew inner pain
to an extent that none of us have suffered or can understand.
That is why he understands us so well.
That is why he is so compassionate.
That is why he is so close to each and every human being.

He comes to each one in their sorrow, their pain,
and he heals them, giving them life.
He does not judge or condemn.
To the woman caught in the act of adultery –
    a fault that could be punished by stoning to death –
he just says: 'I do not condemn you;
        go and sin no more.'

He wants every person to be free from fear
and to grow in love,
to be united to the Father,
Source of all light and love.

He tells the story of the father of the prodigal son,
a father who does not condemn his son,
but takes him in his arms and hugs him for a long time.

Jesus weeps openly with Martha and Mary
because Lazarus has died.
He shows such a delicate sensitivity, such an intense love.
He weeps when we weep
and grieves when we grieve.

Jesus is moved to compassion
as he sees people with all kinds of human infirmities
and sickness
coming to be healed.
He is moved in his guts
(this Greek word for compassion
has a very physical connotation –
implying precisely a movement,
a suffering in one's entrails).
It is as if he cannot keep away from them,
and as though he cannot prevent the healing powers
flowing from him.

Jesus is at home with people who feel rejected and lonely

It is clear from his life
that Jesus feels most at home,
not with the intellectuals or with people in power,
but with the poor, the needy, those in pain,
with those children that his disciples wanted to keep away.
As his ministry progressed
we see him insisting on the privileged place of the poor
in his vision and in his heart:
his option for the poor and for the sinner,

his preferential love for them:
    'When you give a meal,
    do not invite your rich friends and your family,
    for fear that they will invite you back;
    rather invite to a banquet the poor, the lame,
    the sick and the blind.'
    He tells of the King giving a wedding feast for his son.
    All the 'worthy' people invited refuse.
    'Go then into the highways and the byways,'
    he says to his servants,
    'and invite the poor, the lame,
    the sick and the blind.'
    They, of course, accept his invitation with joy!

The poor can be the economically poor,
who are hungry, homeless and out of work,
or the rejected ones –
those put aside because of their infirmities and handicaps,
their apparent uselessness.
They are longing to be accepted and loved,
longing for meaning and a healing relationship.
The poor are those caught up in sin,
yet craving also to be liberated from it.
The poor are also any of us
who are sad and alone, feeling guilty and unloved.
The poor know their own emptiness.
They do not hide from it.
They long for a saviour
who will heal their hearts
and bring them peace.

Of course there are always some in pain and distress,
who shut themselves up in anger and fear;
their hearts are closed to Jesus,
and to his healing promise.
On either side of Jesus, at his crucifixion, were two thieves.
One, whom we call the good thief,
was open to the truth and new life;

45

but the other was angry and turned in upon himself,
and so could receive nothing.

This option for the poor
is not to say that Jesus loves some people more than others,
but rather that he rejoices
with those who open their hearts to him,
and cry out to him.
They recognize who he is:
a person of love and compassion, a healer of hearts.
They welcome him and his message of love;
they have time to listen to him and to rejoice in him.

The rich often seem to be too busy:
they think they have everything they need;
they feel self-sufficient;
they do not need him,
for often they are not really in contact
with their own brokenness,
and their priorities
are seldom in personal relationships and acts of love.
They create a false world
made up of pretence and appearance
rather than of true encounters.
They have no time to waste on Jesus.
They have better things to do:
making and defending wealth, exercising power!
The call of Jesus to universal love
is too great a threat to them.
He spends so much of his time with the outcast,
the riffraff, the dregs of society;
it is easy for the rich to disdain him.

Jesus is not struggling to climb the ladder of promotion.
He does not want to rule in society
and to get the apparently best place,

46

a place where he can exercise power,
even if it is to do good.
No, he is always going down the ladder, closer to the earth,
closer to people, whoever and wherever they may be.
All Jesus wants
is to give his heart and his healing and saving love
to each person,
to become a lover of each person.
Jesus is just *person*-orientated.
He cannot be in a world that lives off appearances
and makes people hide behind barriers and roles.
Jesus keeps going to people where they are
and where they need him most.

The religious leaders of his time
were filled with anger and jealousy.
They could not accept his authority
or his freedom,
which transcended the laws they upheld.
They could not concede his power to forgive sins.
They could not acknowledge
that he was the Christ for whom they had been waiting.
They did not judge him by the fruits of his life
but from the perspective of their theories and doctrines,
so often permeated by their pride and jealousy:
'He cannot be the Christ because . . . '
So they planned to kill him.

During his last paschal meal
Jesus goes even further
in his mission to meet and love people,
to touch them.
He takes water in a basin, and a towel.
He stoops down and washes the feet
of each one of his disciples.
He no longer addresses their intelligence, their heads,
but bends down lower than they
to wash what is lowest and dirtiest,

what is closest to the earth:
he washes their feet.
This gesture coming from the one
who is a leader and teacher
is disgraceful, incomprehensible!
Peter reacts violently.
He would have been ready to wash the feet of Jesus,
to be his servant,
but he could not accept Jesus washing *his* feet,
like a common slave!
Jesus tells him that, if he cannot accept it,
then all is over between them.
Yes, Jesus does not hesitate to manifest his love
in the humble gesture of caring for that part of the body
which is most despised.
He must have washed the feet of Judas
with such tenderness and forgiveness:
Jesus forgiving and asking forgiveness –
not by words but with his body.
It is through his body that he announces
that nothing on earth is so unworthy
it cannot be included in the kingdom of love,
and that all may become part of the wholeness
which radiates from his body.

But so many want to get rid of him:
 pharisees, scribes and elders who are threatened
 and frightened,
 Romans who are annoyed by a stupid fanatical Jew
 stirring up the people,
 rich people who do not want
 to give up their possessions and confess their needs,
 publicans and sinners
 who do not want to change their ways,
 Judas who is eaten up with jealousy.

In the broken body of our world
there are so many people with vested interests

in the brokenness born of fear and conflict:
even enemies come together
to prevent wholeness and healing,
to destroy the promise of light.
In every person
there is a part that is afraid of healing,
that does not want change –
a brokenness with which one has learned to live
and which seems safer than the unknown.

So Jesus begins to make the passage
from the one who is healer
    to the one who is wounded;
from the man of compassion
    to the man in need of compassion;
from the man who cries out:
'If anyone thirsts let him come to me to drink,'
    to the man who cries out:
    'I thirst.'
From announcing the good news to the poor,
Jesus becomes the poor.
He crosses over the boundary line of humanity
which separates those whose needs are satisfied
from those who are broken and cry out in need.

Meanwhile the forces of darkness and evil gather.
Suddenly Jesus becomes the focus of all hatred.
The innocent one becomes the scapegoat,
the cause of all fear,
the source of all danger,
the one who must be broken and destroyed.
This is the moment for which Satan
has been waiting.

Jesus enters fully, freely,
into the agony of his passion.
In the Garden of Gethsemane
the pain of all creation

comes to the surface
in the consciousness of Jesus.
He suffers greatly from the knowledge
that he is to be hurt and killed by his own people –
those he loves and came to save,
those to whom he longed to bring life
in abundance.
But he does not respond with anger or resentment.

He suffers even more from the realization
that his friends have not understood him,
nor all that he has been revealing of the Father:
they have lost trust and abandoned him.
His sweat is like blood
but his heart has no bitterness;
he knows their vulnerability and weakness.

His body quivers and trembles in agony.
In himself, he has no more strength.
He prays to the Father:
'I cannot cope any more –
but not my will, yours be done!'

He is taken before the high priests and elders
and condemned.
They pass him on to Pilate and the Romans –
like a ball in a game.
O the terrible collusion between
the leaders of religion and the state
when they are united against the poor!
Then Jesus hears the crowd yell:
'Crucify him' –
that fickle crowd which a few days earlier had cried out:
'Hosanna, Hosanna to the Son of David, King of Israel!'

The soldiers whip him with cords
to which pieces of metal have been fixed;

his flesh is ripped and torn.
They place a crown of thorns on his head.
They laugh at him,
bending their knees mockingly in front of him.
Around him are soldiers,
cursing and spitting,
hitting the most tender parts of his body.
But no hatred generates in him
in response to all this.

Then he is made to stagger through the streets of Jerusalem
with the heavy log of wood on his lacerated shoulders,
blinded with blood from the wounds on his head.
Some people laugh;
others sneer.
He falls.
Simon of Cyrene is pulled out of the crowd to help him.
The soldiers only fear he might not make it to the hill
but die there in the street instead.

A few women weep
while the disciples, sick with pain, fear and guilt,
are scattered.
And thus his body, racked with pain,
is led outside the walls of Jerusalem.
Yes, out of the beloved city,
the city of David,
the city of God,
He is strung up and nailed to a cross.
Mockingly they say:
'You saved others, now save yourself!'
They cheer and guffaw in derision.

And Jesus cries out:
'I thirst.'
'I need water!'
'I need love.'

'My God, my God, why have you abandoned me?'

His broken body hangs on the wood
> limp
> dirty
> covered with blood
> ugly with wounds;
> his face lined with agony,
> no beauty,
> no comeliness:
> a man of sorrows.

And during all the time he hung there
> the woman was beside him.

Mary was there,
standing at the foot of the cross,
a sign of hope, of trust, of love.
She stood firm,
this silent woman of compassion,
not crushed,
not fleeing from the pain.

Her experience of Jesus was so different
from that of Peter and the other disciples
who had seen his miracles
and witnessed his power and greatness.
They had followed Jesus because of his strength.
Mary's first meeting with Jesus
was in the littleness of his body,
and in the littleness of her body
the day the angel had appeared,
and the Spirit of God had overshadowed her,
when the Word of God was conceived in her womb
in quiet ecstasy.
That night she had slept, bathed in this love,
her heart burning,
her heart awake,

alive with joy:
the Word made flesh in her body.
At that precise moment
God and creation embraced:
a marriage feast was celebrated
in the womb of Mary.

It was fitting and right that she be full of grace,
overshadowed by the Spirit,
to love her child –
not clutching at him out of her own emptiness
with possessive love,
but loving him from the overflowing of her own fullness.
And in this grace she could know and hold him
in all his littleness and vulnerability.
She could respond to his cry for food
and for the food of love
to nourish his gentle heart
hungry for love, for communion and relationship.

So when he was led to the slaughter,
like a lamb, on Calvary
she was not scandalized nor felt ashamed.
She loved him and could be wholly with him,
as he cried out in pain and agony.
She understood his cry, 'I thirst',
'I thirst for love'.
But she did not pray for a healing or a miracle
that the pain would cease,
or that in one loud clap of thunder or flash of lightning
all would be well
and he would be off that cross,
a glorious and triumphant emperor!
Neither did she weep for herself,
agonizing over what tomorrow would bring
without the presence of her beloved.

She trusted without understanding

that this was his way,
this was the hour for which he had come,
the hour of which he had spoken so mysteriously at Cana.
And in this hour she is with him
offering to him her heart, her being, her body,
her gentle and compassionate love,
all that she is;
offering to the Father, with him in his sacrifice,
her life and love
for the healing of our broken world.

It is important to listen to this gentle woman
so silent and compassionate,
for she alone entered the secret of the new meaning of pain.

From the cross Jesus looked at her with such love,
hardly able to see because of the blood and the pain,
and said, 'Woman, here is your son.'
Then he looked at the disciple, John,
the only one to stay with her,
and he said: 'Here is your mother.'

In the pain flowing from his own body
he linked this woman, his mother,
to John,
in a covenant of love.

Before he died,
he cried out: 'Father,
        forgive them.
        They do not know what they are doing!'
In that moment
he transformed the violence of human beings
into forgiveness and compassion.
He broke the chain of violence, hatred and sin
which had flowed from generation to generation
from Adam and Eve until today.

Something new *is* being given:
violence *is* changed to forgiveness.
The door of love *is* opening
because of his death.
He yielded up the Spirit
and from his heart pierced by the lance
flowed blood and water;
the living water he had promised
would flow in the Samaritan woman
and in all who believe;
the spring of water welling up
into eternal life;
the waters from the temple
prophesied by Ezekiel –
healing waters,
giving new life,
bearing rich fruit.

But those who were there
saw only his broken body
lying in the lap of the woman.

Then his dead body was taken to a tomb,
and a huge rock was placed over the entrance.

He descended into the earth.
He had to go on descending
into the deepest experience of death,
entering the place of furthest separation from God
until he could descend no further.

It was not easy for the disciples
to believe in the transformation
that was being accomplished.
They knew only that the body of Jesus
was broken and dead.
And they saw that their hearts and their unity
were also in pieces:

Judas has committed suicide;
Peter is hiding in shame and remorse;
two of the disciples,
     judging the reports of women
     that Jesus has been seen alive
     as obviously hysterical,
break from the group and leave for Emmaus.
All of them are crushed by despair.
Their wonderful dream has exploded.
It is all over.
Finished.

Had they not given all for Jesus?
How their friends and family had scoffed at them then,
for being unrealistic.
They had accepted rejection and hardship
for the sake of Jesus.
They had dreamed of a strong Messiah
     overthrowing the powers of oppression,
     setting up the new kingdom
     where they would have a place in the government
     and exercise powers.
They had already had a foretaste during the past three years,
     experiencing in themselves the power
     to chase away devils and heal the sick.
They had witnessed Jesus in his strength
     successfully attracting large crowds,
     speaking with authority,
     accomplishing great signs,
     facing the legalistic traps of the pharisees
     with such skill and genius that they were
     dumbfounded.
The kingdom of love seemed to be at hand.
Sickness, death and injustice would disappear forever!
And they were to be part of this wonderful kingdom.
But now!
That for which they had given their lives
has collapsed.

Everything is broken, even more cruelly than before –
        the body of Jesus,
        their dreams,
        their hearts,
        their power,
        the body of their unity;
        all is broken.
And all this brokenness seems only to reveal
        their own inner decay and despair,
        the inconsolable cry of loneliness,
        the horror and emptiness of death.

Perhaps in running away from this
        they had only been following the powerful,
        the successful Jesus.
Running away from this
        they had been totally unable to listen to him
        when he had spoken quite clearly
        of his impending suffering and death:
            'The son of man will suffer greatly,
            at the hands of the high priests and elders,
            and will be killed.'

Peter had rebuked him:
        'God forbid, this shall never happen to you!'
        'Don't exaggerate, we will defend you!'
It was such a natural response of good-will.
But Jesus had looked at him,
white with anger and inner pain:
        'Get behind me, Satan!'
Peter had sparked something so deep in him:
        'You are an obstacle to me,' Jesus said,
        'Your thoughts are not the thoughts of God
            but of human beings!'

The disciples had not had even an inkling
that the Messiah might be different
from their dream of a strong, powerful king

who would rule with justice.
The idea of a suffering Messiah,
a suffering servant
was repulsive.

That is why, during the trial of Jesus,
Peter could say to the servant women,
'I do not know that man.'
'I DO NOT KNOW THAT MAN.'
It was true!
He did not know him.
He did not know the Jesus who is little and vulnerable,
    the Jesus who weeps and is overwhelmed by pain,
    the Jesus who experiences
    rejection and human suffering.

Jesus is risen

Even while the disciples are plunged into total despair
the body of Jesus is being resurrected.
On the third day
they see him,
and hear his voice.
They touch him and even see him eating in front of them.
How is it possible?
They cannot believe their eyes and ears!
But it really is Jesus.
They are astounded,
filled with joy
but also pain because of their lack of trust,
their shameful cowardice.
They do not know whether to sing or cry.
But Jesus has only one message:
    'Shalom, peace.'
His look of love
is a gentle smile,
without condemnation.

58

It is only at Pentecost
as they pray together
with Mary, the Mother,
waiting for the promise,
that they really begin to understand
the full meaning of brokenness
     and the gift of the broken body of Jesus;
they begin to understand why he had shown them
     imprinted in his body, now healed and restored,
     his wounds, open but no longer bleeding,
and why he had invited Thomas to put his hand
in the side where the lance had pierced.

As the Spirit filled them
with inner fire and light,
they could enter at last
into the mystery of the lamb.
They could comprehend the secret song
of the Suffering Servant:

'He had no form or comeliness that we should look at him,
    and no beauty that we should desire him.
He was despised and rejected by men;
    a man of sorrows, and acquainted with grief;
and as one from whom men hide their faces
    he was despised, and we esteemed him not.
Surely he has borne our griefs
    and carried our sorrows;
yet we esteemed him stricken,
    smitten by God and afflicted.
But he was wounded for our transgressions,
    he was bruised for our iniquities;
upon him was the chastisement that made us whole,
    and with his stripes we are healed.'

It was through his littleness and pain,
his brokenness and death,
that Jesus had saved them,

by conquering sin and death and the power of the Evil One.
He had overcome violence,
not by shunning or ignoring it,
but by receiving it
and then transforming it
into tenderness and forgiveness.

By his broken body,
we, the body of humanity,
are made whole,
whoever we are and wherever we are,
whatever our doubts or shame,
our turmoil or anger.
We are healed and can come together
in the fullness of the Body of Christ.

He has penetrated into the depths of darkness,
loneliness, rejection, agony and fear,
in order to touch the depths of darkness
in each one of us
and to call us to belief,
to call us to walk in this world of darkness,
loneliness, rejection, agony and fear –
hoping, trusting in the resurrection.

The secret meaning of brokenness is revealed

By his passion, death and resurrection
Jesus brings to the world
a new meaning to suffering and pain,
to weakness and vulnerability.

We are freed from the idea
that suffering and pain are punishments for our evil ways,
and discover instead that they lead us
along the road to glory and liberation.

Our brokenness is the wound

through which the full power of God
can penetrate our being
and transfigure us in him.

Loneliness is not something from which we must flee
but the place from where we can cry out to God,
where he will find us and we can find him.

Yes, through our wounds
the power of God can penetrate us
and become like rivers of living water
to irrigate the arid earth within us.
Thus we may irrigate the arid earth of others,
so that hope and love are reborn.

Jesus wants us not only to live in him
and he in us,
he also invites us to share in his redeeming act,
to be with him on the cross,
giving life to the world.

This is the amazing gift of God.
This is the ultimate meaning of suffering,
pain and brokenness:
that our suffering, hidden in the brokenness of Jesus,
can become a source of wholeness for the Church,
for the world,
and for each person
in and through the risen body of Christ
with its new and total wholeness.

Often our experience in life
is of being pulled between two poles:
the poles of ecstasy and pain,
the glory and the cross:
    our hearts are lifted up
    in the splendour of the cathedral
    with the sound of heavenly music,

the awareness of sacred space,
the consciousness of centuries
giving glory to the majesty of God.

Our hearts are stricken in pain
before the world of apparently meaningless suffering,
hunger,
imprisonment,
death,
children killed in the womb,
people denied their most fundamental rights,
people tortured
or driven from their land,
people dying without dignity.
We too are lost in our own confusion,
our inner conflicts or doubts.
Each of us is called to experience both ecstasy and pain,
shunning neither one nor the other,
but entering into that mystery
where one leads to the other,
where misery and mercy embrace
and wholeness rises from brokenness.

Running away from pain
can never bring joy.
To hide from it,
to pretend it does not exist,
        perhaps drowning our memory of it
        in front of too much television,
or to spend time theorizing about an ideal world
        where pain is eliminated:
all this is only illusion.

So, do not shrink from suffering,
but enter into it
and discover there the mystery
of the presence of the risen Jesus.
He is hidden there, in the sacrament of the poor.

And do not turn aside from your own pain,
your anguish and brokenness,
your loneliness and emptiness,
by pretending you are strong.
Go within yourself.
Go down the ladder of your own being
until you discover –
like a seed
buried in the broken, ploughed earth
of your own vulnerability –
the presence of Jesus,
the light shining in the darkness.

This road is not always an easy road to follow.
There will be times of discouragement and anger;
there will be many setbacks,
times of ups and downs,
times of doubt.
But little by little
if you are well accompanied on this journey,
you will begin to see the light in the darkness,
you will drink the water which springs from arid land.

Mary

In order to welcome the gift of the body of Jesus
    we must look more fully at the woman
      who conceived him
      and gave him birth –
      Mary.

For none like her
      enveloped his body,
      touched his body,
      loved his body,

washed his body,
venerated his body.
The body of Christ
flowed from her body,
the fruit of her womb.
It was her body that nourished his body:
her breasts gave
him the energy and nourishment to grow;
her touch protected him
and revealed to him that he was loved;
her presence made him sing with joy;
the light in her eyes called forth the light in his.
Before she was touched and sanctified by his words,
she had been touched and sanctified by his body,
the Temple of God,
the sacred place where God resides.

And she loved his body,
not in a possessive way
flowing from an emptiness.
She loved it from a fullness,
a fullness of grace,
longing that it might grow,
and that her Beloved might in everything fulfil
the will of the Father.

For thirty years she was close to his body,
feeding it,
and being nourished by his presence,
the real presence.
For thirty years she was made holy and whole
by the gentle, silent body of Jesus,
through which was revealed
the light of his inner beauty,
the presence of the Father in him,
the body of Jesus, so infinitely sensitive
to the pain and beauty of all creation.

Mary loved this tender body of her son,
but her love was poured out even more
as she beheld the broken body of Christ.
Her love flowed then
from her heart pierced by the sword,
her wound, her terrible wound
crying grief, weeping over
      the body of Jesus torn apart,
      spat upon and scourged,
      crowned with thorns,
      disfigured by pain and blood;
she wept over
      the body nailed to the wood,
      the body pierced by a lance;
she wept over her people
who, in rejecting Jesus,
were wounding themselves.
She loved his body as it lay dead upon her lap,
she touched this wounded, crushed body with love,
she touched his wounds in veneration,
she loved his body as it lay silent and alone in the tomb –
crying forgiveness for her people.

O gentle woman,
      on that night of the resurrection
      was not your body awoken
      by the risen body of the one you loved?

Nowhere is spoken of the meeting between you
and the risen Jesus.
It is the secret hidden in your heart.
But did he not come to awaken your being
from the torpor of pain and separation?
Did he not come to end that terrible time of waiting
as you watched for the third day,
not knowing,
but trusting
in love?

O gentle woman, did not your body then
quiver in gentle ecstasy
as the fire of love broke forth in you,
when the risen body of Christ
revealed itself – not outside you –
but inside?
You did not need to see him,
for it was from within that your heart leapt forth.

As on the day you conceived the Son of God,
that day when you were alone in Nazareth,
and lived for the first time the ecstasy
of being in union
with the body of Christ:
so too, on this day in Jerusalem
or nearby, maybe in Bethany,
your body quivered in greater ecstasy,
your flesh was transfigured in a new and deeper way.

It is no wonder that Elizabeth,
moved by the Spirit when she welcomed you
after she had conceived John,
cried out;
      'Blessed are you among women
      and blessed is the fruit of your womb.'

And you yourself burst into song:
      'My soul glorifies the Lord
      and my spirit exults in God my saviour,
      for he has looked upon the lowliness of his servant.
      From henceforth all generations will call me blessed
      for the Almighty has done great things in me
      and holy is his name.'

Yes, from thenceforth all have called you blessed,
O gentle woman,
They have honoured you and loved you,
and rightly so;

lead us along the road
that we may know Jesus
and love him, as you knew and loved him.

O silent woman
    clothe us in your silence
    and the silence of the Trinity,
    where love
    is presence,
    communion,
    and gift of self.

O compassionate woman,
    who stood by the broken and naked body of Jesus,
    your heart crushed and in agony,
    your eyes filled with tears,
    teach us compassion for this broken world of ours.

O gentle woman,
    when so many today are looking for gurus
    to lead them in the path of God,
    lead us
    in the silent ways of Jesus.

The Call to Wholeness in the Body of Christ

By his death and resurrection
Jesus came to bring together
this fragmented world of ours.

He came to transform fear into trust,
so that the walls separating people into enemies
would disappear,
and we could join together in a covenant of love,
    'So shall we fully grow up into Christ,
    who is the head,
    and by whom the whole body

is bonded and knit together,
every joint adding its own strength
for each individual part to work according to its
function,
so the whole body grows until it has built itself up in
love.' ·

Yes, this is the vision of Jesus for our world
announced by St Paul:
one body –
with the poorest and weakest among us at the heart,
those that we judge the most despicable, honoured;
where each person is important
because all are necessary.
His body, to which we all belong
joined in love,
filled with the Spirit.
This is the kingdom.

That is why Jesus had to leave this world.
He had to go
so that we could become Jesus,
continuing his work
of announcing the good news to the poor
and of healing the body of humanity
that is still so broken;
completing in our own flesh his passion,
being men and women of peace,
reconciling people, one to another
because we are reconciled with the Father;
bridging the gap that separates rich and poor,
building networks of friendship
founded on the rock of love,
creating oases of hope ·
where healing waters flow
and fruits are borne.

Today as yesterday
Jesus is calling us to follow him,
to walk in his footsteps.

He is calling you and me to be like him,
wherever and whoever we are,
whatever we think of ourselves.
>To live as he lived,
>to love as he loved,
>to speak as he spoke
>to offer our lives as he offered his,
>to do what he did,
>to do even greater things
>because of his going to the Father.

By ourselves this is impossible.
How can we live and love as he did,
except through the mysterious gift and power
which he gives us through his Spirit,
so that we become his face, his hands, his heart and body?

Not just you and I alone, as individuals,
but together in the body of community.
And again not a group, separated and isolated,
thinking it is the best
and sufficient unto itself,
but linked to others,
to other communities,
all cells of the one body, the Church,
united with men and women all over the world.

Jesus is calling us
>to speak the truth as he did,
>to become compassionate
>and to walk down the ladder
>>into the heart of poverty and pain,
>>both our own and that of others.
There we will find the freedom
to cherish all the beauty given us,
the love, and song, and laughter,
and we will then rise up together
in a community of forgiveness and celebration
>knowing what it is to be his Body.

Part III
Restoring the Broken Body to Wholeness

My brother, my sister,
you who are called to follow Jesus,
to become a man or a woman of peace
in this divided world of ours,
may I give you some words of hope
to help you along your journey?

From an early age I was involved in the business of war.
I learnt how to use guns and machines of destruction,
how to be quick and efficient
in order to destroy the enemy before we were destroyed.
But Jesus called me to leave the things of war
for the things of peace
and to follow him.

I put myself at the feet of a holy priest,
receiving the gift of prayer
and attending to the word of God.
I studied philosophy and theology,
and later began to teach philosophy.
I did all this,
my generosity tainted with my pride,
covering over my brokenness, weakness, and my sin;

but I trusted and I walked, though sometimes falteringly,
        with Jesus.

Then Jesus led me
to men and women who have a mental handicap.
I had never met them before.
I was amazed by this first meeting.
I sensed the primal cry
coming from their broken bodies, hearts and minds,
        'Do you love me?
         Am I lovable?
        Have I any value?
        Why have I been abandoned?'
Encouraged by the holy priest,
I began to live with two men
whom I had met in a terrible asylum.
Their parents had died so they were alone
with no one to welcome them.
They were angry at all that had happened to them.
They lived partly in a world of dreams,
trying to escape the pain in them.
They were hungry for love and meaning.

We began to live together.
I did some of the cooking.
We did not eat very well!
But we shared and laughed together.
We got angry with each other too!
I made mistakes
through ignorance and lack of experience.
I treated them too much like children,
telling them what to do,
not really listening to them
or respecting the light hidden in their hearts.
But I began to learn through all the mistakes I made.
And little by little we became friends
and trust was born between us.

71

They began to lead me
into the world of healing relationships.

People came to help.
Together we welcomed more people,
and so l'Arche grew.
We bought other houses in the village;
other communities began in different parts of the world.
Now we are a big family in many countries.
And it is the people who are handicapped
who are at the heart of our communities.
Though they are sometimes angry, violent,
weak and broken,
it is they who have taught me how to live and to love,
        who have taught me about pain and suffering,
        who have taught me about Jesus and the Church,
        and who are teaching me still how to follow Jesus.

This way is open to us all.
Jesus calls some to leave everything
and to become beggars of compassion like St Francis.
He invites others to leave their familiar surroundings
to share their lives fully with the poor and weak.
Still others, he calls to invite an elderly neighbour,
or a child with a handicap,
into their hearts and their homes.
Jesus calls each one of us to go deeper,
and to be compassionate as he was compassionate,
wherever we find ourselves,
and whatever our circumstances.

The poor and the weak have revealed to me
the great secret of Jesus.
If you wish to follow him
you must not try to climb the ladder of success and power,
becoming more and more important.
Instead, you must walk *down* the ladder,
to meet and walk with people

who are broken and in pain.
The light is there, shining in the darkness,
in the darkness of their poverty.
The poor with whom you are called to share your life
are perhaps the sick and the old;
people out of work,
young people caught up in the world of drugs,
people angry because they were terribly hurt
when they were young,
people with disabilities or sick with Aids,
or just out of prison;
people in slums or ghettos,
people in far-off lands
where there is much hunger and suffering,
people who are oppressed
because of the colour of their skin,
people who are lonely in overcrowded cities,
people in pain.

Christians have always proclaimed
the need to serve the poor,
to do things that will help them
rise up out of their misery.
But what are we discovering at l'Arche
is that those who are poor possess a precious gift
and that we must listen to them with deep respect.
They have a gift for others.
We are discovering too
that the life-giving Jesus is hidden in them.
He is truly there.
If you become a friend of the poor,
you become a friend of Jesus.

If you enter into a close relationship
with those who are poor,
you enter into an intimate relationship with Jesus
and you will be led into the heart of the beatitudes.
Jesus spoke truly when he said:

'Whatsoever you do to the least of your brethren
you do unto me.'
'Whosoever welcomes one of these little ones
in my name welcomes me,
and whosoever welcomes me
welcomes the one who sent me.'
Yet it seems so impossible that the Father should be revealed
in the anguished face of a child.
Who is this God
who resides in the broken heart of a child?

If you enter into relationship
with a lonely or suffering person
you will discover something else:
that it is you who are being healed.
The broken person will reveal to you your own hurt
and the hardness of your heart,
but *also* how much *you* are loved.
Thus the one you came to heal
becomes your healer.

If you let yourself be moulded thus
by the cry of the poor
and accept their healing friendship,
then they may guide your footsteps into community
and lead you into a new vision of humanity,
a new world order,
not governed by power and fear
but where the poor and the weak are at the centre.
They will lead you into the kingdom Jesus speaks of.

As people join together in a covenant
within a community,
they begin to discover what it means
to be a peace-maker in a broken world.
Above all they discover
that there is hope.

They are not condemned to brokenness,
but can struggle for peace together.

Your life and mine have a meaning
in the heart of Jesus
and, by the power of the holy Spirit,
we can bring life to the world
through little acts of love and faithful relationships.

Now, as never before, we must try to bridge the gap
that separates people,
cultures, races, religions, rich and poor.
Conflict is too dangerous a game;
war can lead us only to annihilation.
Jesus calls us to follow him
to help bridge the gap –
especially the great chasm of fear –
and so become peace-makers like him.

You might find yourself leaving your culture
to live with people
who are rejected and in pain –
then, no doubt, you will be called 'utopian'.
People will say your feet are not on the ground.
There will be many obstacles
to prevent you from meeting the poor
and discovering the mystery of healing in them.

There will even be those in the Church
who will say you are choosing a path
that is too radical, too hard, too this or too that.
They will suggest that you need to study theology,
unaware that the poor are the best teachers in theology,
if we can learn to listen to them.

Others will say that you will get burnt out;
and they will be right,
unless you go deep enough

in welcoming the gift of this call
with wisdom.

Today there are so many manifestations of division.
There is a danger of pious people
praying in warm communities,
worrying about their spiritual life
but not welcoming the poor or the hungry;
seemingly unaware of the depth of pain around them.
They seem unable to recognize
the power of the Spirit given to them
and their capacity to be true peace-makers.

And then there are others working for the poor,
seeking to liberate them,
but they have forgotten the power of prayer
and the healing presence of Jesus.
Identifying themselves with the poor
they may become full of hatred
towards those who have riches and power,
or be consumed with anger
against political and economic structures,
prepared even to kill.

Can we not bridge the gap
and discover Jesus, Prince of Peace,
calling us each one of us
to be peace-makers,
bringing together in love
people with all their differences.

Meeting Brokenness with Respect

As people leave their family, culture and familiar ways
following, like Abraham, the call of God,
to go to an unfamiliar land,

they will begin to discover those who are different,
who are broken in their bodies
and in their hearts;
they will suffer loss and experience a time of grief.
It is not easy for them to let go of their security
and to enter a world which is different
and which is so full of pain.

There is a temptation then to avoid facing it
by *doing* many things,
to cover up feelings of loneliness and insecurity.
There is always this danger of throwing oneself into work
in order to feel useful, appreciated, and wanted.

It is important to take time
and not rush into things.
There are many forms of culture shock,
so people need to be patient and gentle with themselves.
People need to be reminded
that they have not come so much to *do* things
as to learn to be,
and that they must not come
like a mechanic with tools of knowledge and theory
to repair what is broken.

They must come to discover a secret,
like a treasure hidden in a field,
the pearl of great price.
Or as a child about to receive a marvellous gift –
    a gift of relationship,
    a gift of friendship,
    the gift of light, love and wisdom
    hidden in the hearts of the poor and the lonely,
    the sick and the blind,
    in all those who are vulnerable
    and have nothing to lose.
So they must come, as a child in wonder.

For many the first moment of wonderment will be painful:
they have come to serve the poor;
    to do good and be generous;
    to follow Jesus;
    to feed the hungry;
or they have just welcomed into their home
    a child with a handicap –
    and all they receive is a slap in the face,
    rejection, anger.

Do not be surprised at rejection by broken people.
They have suffered a great deal
    at the hands
    of the knowledgeable and the powerful –
    doctors, psychologists, sociologists, social workers,
    politicians, the police and others.
They have suffered so much from broken promises,
from people wanting to learn from experiments
or to write a thesis
and then, having gained what they wanted –
votes, recognition, an impressive book or article –
going away and never coming back.

Rejected people are sick and tired
    of 'good' and 'generous' people,
    of people who claim to be Christians,
    of people who come to them
    on their pedestals of pride and power
    to do them good.
No wonder their hearts are closed to new people.
They are waiting
    for someone who really cares
    and who sees in them the light of love and wisdom,
    who recognizes their gifts and their beauty;
    someone who will accept them just as they are
    with no preconceived ideas
    that they should change.
They are waiting

for someone who accepts their need to be changed,
one who is willing to know the pain of growth
and who can become vulnerable enough to love,
and so discover the pearl of great price.

When Jesus meets the woman of Samaria,
he does not begin by speaking to her
from the top of a pedestal,
but from the pit of his own needs – his cry of thirst:
    'Give me to drink.'
She belonged to what we call 'the fourth world':
    She had lived with five men
    and the man she was then living with
    was not her husband.
 She was utterly broken:
        her self-image shattered,
        ridden with guilt,
        rejected by her own people
        who were themselves rejected.
Jesus looks at this woman,
whom others scoff at and despise,
the 'dirty prostitute',
and he says:
        'You can do something for me,
        I need your help.'

The ways of God
are to bring down the powerful from their thrones
and to lift up the lowly;
not to judge or condemn
but to meet people where they are
and to give life.

To give life
is to be full of sacred wonder and reverence
in front of the mystery of the person;
it is to see the beauty
within and beyond all that is broken.

To love is not to give of your riches
but to reveal to others their riches, their gifts, their value,
and to trust them and their capacity to grow.

So it is important to approach people
in their brokenness and littleness
gently,
so gently,
not forcing yourself upon them,
but accepting them as they are,
with humility and respect.

The Basis of Dialogue

If you wish to enter the world of those
who are broken or closed in upon themselves,
it is important to learn their language.

Learning a language
is not just learning French or Spanish or German.
It is learning to understand what people are really saying,
the non-verbal as well as the verbal language.
The verbal, exterior language is the beginning
and is absolutely necessary,
but you must go deeper
and discover what it means to listen:
to listen deeply to another,
to the cry flowing from the heart,
in order to understand people,
both in their pain and in their gift;
to understand what they are truly asking
so that you can hold their wound, their pain
and all that flows from it:
  violence, anger or depression,
  self-centredness and limitless demands;

the suffocating urge to possess,
     the refusal to let go;
to accept these with compassion,
without judging, without condemning.

You must go deeper and discover
what it really means to see another!
     – to see the light shining in the darkness,
     – to recognize the seeds of hidden gifts
     and to water these seeds and rejoice as they grow.
You may also discover what it really means to give:
     to give to another the possibility
     to take on more responsibility;
     to give to another hope and trust,
     acceptance of his or her essential beauty,
     and to welcome inner riches as they unfold.
To do this means you must listen and understand
the non-verbal language of the body
as well as the language of words.
The first language of the child is so deep,
this language of the body.
We can perhaps recognize the pain and anguish
conveyed in the taut face, all screwed up, of a tiny baby,
just as we can recognize the peaceful surrender
in its radiance of trust and light.
Some people can only talk with their bodies;
only from there do true words flow.
Sometimes it is because they cannot speak,
but also it may be because they have lost trust in words.
They have heard too often
words that have been only empty promises,
words that have been lies,
words that condemn or despise,
words that hurt.

At the beginning of the Church
on that glorious day of Pentecost,
when the Spirit came like an explosion of new life,
the disciples began to talk in different languages
so that all could hear about Jesus in their own tongue.
The Spirit does not speak in just one language,
and Christians must not impose theirs.
Language is sacred,
intimately linked to culture,
    to the earth and the climate,
    to the mother.
There is a profound meaning in the fact
that we speak our 'mother tongue'.

The first disciples were given new languages
so that they might understand, right from the beginning,
the ways of God:
    how he wants us to respect difference
    and to learn the language of the other
    so that there may be true communication
    and communion.
This new language is not always given
in a flash of the Spirit, alas!
We must learn it
and this implies hard work!
Learn and respect others in their own culture;
    their ways of eating,
    their ways of interacting,
    their ways of doing things,
    their forms of relationships.
Come, listen and learn.
Do not judge others and their ways;
instead respect them and love them.
Open your hearts to them.

If you come in this way,
open, listening humbly, without judging,
then gradually you will discover

that you are trusted.
Your heart will be touched.
You will begin to discover the secret of communion.

Staying

We find in the communities of l'Arche,
as trust deepens between helpers and those around them,
–whose bodies, minds and hearts
are sometimes terribly broken –
life, new life, will begin to surge,
springing from the very depths,
from the source and centre of their being.
Love,
the capacity to listen, to welcome, to receive,
engenders meaning and hope,
gradually transforming a broken self-image
into a positive one.
By their very presence,
by accepting people as they are,
the helpers become healers.
By the power of affirmation,
people are led to trust in themselves
and to discover their own beauty and riches.
They realize they do not have to hide from others
in anger and sadness;
they are not dirty, ugly or evil.
Through a caring, committed presence,
people will discover
    that they are allowed to be themselves:
    that they are loved and so are lovable;
    that they have gifts
    and their lives have meaning;
    that they can grow and do beautiful things
    and in turn be peace-makers in a world of conflict.

The helper's life will then become fruitful,
not just productive.
We can all *do* things:
produce objects that are beautiful and useful,
and thus receive acclaim.
But in l'Arche communities helpers are called to do more
than produce inanimate objects
which can never talk or relate with each other,
however beautiful and holy their creation may be.
By their love and their tenderness,
their appreciation and their affirmation,
they are called
to *give life* to people who are broken and in despair.

Does not a child give life to its mother,
just as much as the mother gives life to her child?
The child calls forth her maternity,
helps her to discover her secret beauty,
her capacity to soothe, to give peace
and her gift to call forth trust and growth.

As we interact with broken people,
be it in l'Arche or elsewhere,
we enter into this flow of life,
that mutual trust and affirmation between people,
giving life one to another,
discovering our mutual fecundity and fruitfulness.

Jesus told the Samaritan woman
that if she drank the waters he would give her,
the water from the well of his being,
then this water would become in her
a spring welling up in eternal life.
She would then give life to others,
becoming a source of life,
quenching the thirst of others:
her life would no longer be sterile
but would bear much fruit.

84

People would be able to say:
'Blessed is the fruit of your being!'
And Jesus is speaking to the Samaritan woman
in each one of us:
to that broken part of our being where there is such fear
and where we have no confidence
in our ability to love and be loved,
'You are called to bear much fruit,
to be no longer sterile but fecund.'

When Jesus cried out in the temple,
he cried out to all of us and to all of humanity:
'If anyone thirsts,
let him come to me and drink;
as Scriptures says,
"he who believes in me,
rivers of living waters will flow from his belly!" '
Jesus was speaking of the Spirit
that had not yet been given,
for Jesus had not yet been glorified.

For so many people at l'Arche
this is a rich and new experience.
They have always been told to excel and be productive.
At home they have perhaps experienced aggression
or a possessive, guilt-making love,
not the freedom to be themselves and to grow.
At work, in school,
they have had to fulfil the expectations of others;
they have been in a world of competition and rivalry,
and if they did not succeed,
they felt left behind, incapable of winning;
they fell into another world of sadness, perhaps sulking,
becoming depressed
or seeking compensation in superficial sexual relationships,
losing themselves in the world of drink, drugs or films,
or daring each other to acts of folly.

But, when they discover
that through their caring love and affirmation
they can give life to others,
they feel something entirely new:
> an experience of mutual trust and communion,
> presence one to another
> becoming healers of each other.

Their bodies, their beings become whole again;
hope begins to flow.
This becomes also a gentle experience
of the presence of God
in themselves
and in the other.
There is a taste of the Trinity,
a deep sharing in the thirst of Jesus:
> 'That they may be one, as the Father and I are one,
> that they may be totally one.'
But all this is so fragile;
this experience of communion is so tenuous
in the face of the forces opposing it
in and around us:
> the incessant noise of the mass media;
> the fear of what others think and say;
> the seduction of riches and power;
> the provocation of a perverted sexuality;
> the atmosphere of fear and aggression.
All this can so easily stifle
the beauty of the tiny flower
emerging in the vulnerable earth of our being.

That is why we often need someone to help us interpret
the beauty and the depths of this experience,
however tenuous or fragile it may be;
to assure us that it is truly an experience
of the presence of God,
to encourage us to be still and listen
to the gift that is being given;

to remind us to 'Be still and know that I am your God'.
It is something new.
In this experience of communion,
there will be no acquisitions
no diplomas to vouch for it,
no end-product,
nothing visible to hold on to,
no acclamation;
just a gentle experience of love and of the presence of God.
Dare I say it?
Yes, it can even be a mystical experience,
something so deep, so fragile
that if you are not careful
you can walk on it,
    crush it,
    ignore it
    or pass it by.
Yet it is the gentle call of Jesus,
the touch of his hands,
a new love being born.

It is something that springs from the source of your being,
melting from inside the coating of ice and coldness;
gently dismantling the carefully built barriers
that have been constructed
around the vulnerability of your heart
because of fear.

It is like the rebirth of the child within you:
the gentle, tender, vulnerable, fragile child,
hidden deep within you,
that has been clouded over
by your need to prove yourself,
to be adult, clever, intelligent, acclaimed;
or by your need to defend yourself against others
and their exaggerated expectations of you.
Perhaps it is your first experience of what Jesus said
as he was moved by the Spirit:

'Blessed are you, Father,
Lord of heaven and earth;
You have hidden these things
from the clever and the intelligent
and revealed them to little ones.'

Jesus does not come in the thunder and the lightning;
nor does he come in the wild wind.
He comes in the gentle breeze of the evening.
The Spirit blows so quietly over our earth.
If we are not attentive,
we run the risk of not recognizing the presence of God
manifested in our lives.
For he is a gentle God,
a tender, loving God,
coming to give life so quietly,
        far from the world of pride and cleverness,
        far from the pedestals of power and administration,
        far from the self-satisfaction, defence mechanisms
        and security of the self-sufficient.
He is hidden in the cave of our being.

What so many receive in l'Arche
in those moments of gentle communion,
can also be the experience of a mother with her child,
or someone who becomes a real friend of another who is
suffering or lonely.

Courage to Face a Deeper Pain

In the beauty and fragility of this experience
lies also its pain.
In awakening our capacity to love,
it awakens what is deepest in us
which includes our vulnerability and sensitivity.
For the dismantled barriers permit the rising

not only of the waters of new life,
but also of the forces of darkness,
    our need to possess,
    our desire to hold on to people to fill our emptiness,
    the eruption of jealousy
    and with it the capacity to hate.
Love is gentle and beautiful
but there comes with it a terrible fear:
    fear of the future
        and of the risk of getting too involved;
    fear that it will lead only to the death
        of our so-called freedom,
    fear too of being hurt,
        for to love is to become vulnerable;
        to love is always a risk.

When we produce something,
the result is tangible;
we possess the object and the glory.
When we give life to others,
we enter into risk and insecurity,
for we do not possess an object
and we have no glory.
There is only trust and communion with the other person
with whom we discover bonds of love,
a covenant,
given by God.
We become pilgrims,
walking in a beautiful land,
not sure where it will lead.
We can be sure only of love
and of the presence of God,
the call to surrender,
and to be guided by faithful love.

Whenever we come together with broken people,

other pains more terrible and more frightening
come to the surface,
springing from the depths of our being.
Between the gentle moments of communion and trust
are other moments
– perhaps when we are tired, uncentred,
feeling lost and confused –
when the broken person close to us
provokes us,
screams for something we cannot give,
either because our well is drying up and we feel empty
or because the person in front of us
asks for too much.
(How can we be father, mother, husband or wife, friend,
      brother, sister and child
      to another person
      who is hungry for all those relationships?)

And then we discover something surging up within us
which we never suspected:
      an anger or an anguish,
      a need to hit or hurt.
It is the same feeling some parents can feel
in front of their provocative or crying child,
at a moment when their inner well is dried up:
      feelings that can lead to the injury of children,
      so frequent that we now speak
      of the 'battered-child syndrome'.

The violence, fears and needs of some broken people
can arouse our violence and fears:
      a terrible power surges forth,
      not to hold with firmness,
      but to hurt, to wound, to break.
Something over which we have no control:
      the terrifying powers of darkness in us;
      our capacity to hurt and even to kill a weaker person!

The anguish of the broken
can arouse our anguish:
    a terrible feeling of confusion,
    inner agitation
    a sense of death and emptiness.

The quiet grace of communion has disappeared
– was it only an illusion? –
and is now replaced
by an overwhelming inner turmoil and pain:
    the discovery of our own terrible brokenness,
    hidden under our capacity to do things,
    hidden under our knowledge and intelligence,
    hidden under our casualness,
    security and good humour,
    hidden even under our works of piety
    and times of prayer.

In that fleeting moment,
we touch our own darkness – so deep and so terrible.
We can either run away,
finding all sorts of excuses and rational arguments
for leaving people in pain,
completely withdrawing
from these newly formed relationships:
not daring to speak with anyone
about this terrible experience,
trying to forget it, yet feeling guilty.
Or else we can face what lies within,
and discover who we really are.
Beneath the appearance of cheerful generosity,
under that image of goodness
we have allowed others to have of us
and have perhaps even fostered,
we are really no more than a broken person
in need of healing.
This moment can be a moment of salvation,
a turning point of growth towards wholeness.

But it is not easy;
so great is the temptation
to flee from the reality of our being.
We need a gentle guide
who can help us to interpret the pain
and to understand what is happening.
This is an important moment,
a passage in our spiritual journey,
when we will be reborn in truth.
It is a humiliating experience
but also an experience of truth.
It is better to know who we really are,
with the darkness inside us
and then to accept and face up to it,
than to pretend it does not exist
and to arrange our lives in such a way
that this darkness remains hidden.
Then it will only fester
and will govern our lives on an unconscious level,
until eventually it surfaces in another form.

In the story of the prodigal son,
the elder son was not aware of the darker parts of his being.
That is why he judged his younger brother,
and criticized his father,
and was incapable of compassion.

The explosion of anguish leads us to poverty and humility.
It is this recognition of our brokenness and of our wounds
which takes us off our pedestal:
in our own eyes, and sometimes in the eyes of others,
we have been plunged into the pit.
But if we are helped,
we can discover the gift of these truths:
    we are no different from those we try to serve;
    we too are broken and wounded like them;
    in a way we had not realized before
    we are truly together brothers and sisters;

we are a wounded people;
we can love each other, forgive each other
and celebrate together our oneness.
Perhaps we can only truly accept this humiliation
if we live an experience similar to the one
lived by the prodigal son.
If we discover that we are loved and forgiven
and accepted by the Father
just as we are,
in all our brokenness,
with all the darkness and pain inside us,
then we too can weep in the arms of God,
rejoicing in his forgiveness.

Yes the cry and the anguish of the poor
triggers off our own cry and anguish;
we touch our point of pain and helplessness.

But then we discover the new name of God,
the name revealed by Jesus,
of the Spirit, the Holy Spirit;
the Father will send a *Paraclete*.
It is a beautiful name,
meaning literally
'the one who answers the cry or the call',
like a mother
who takes in her arms her weeping child.
She is a paraclete.
The name of God is
'the one who answers the cry'.
Mercy and misery embrace!
We can only know the incredible mercy and love of God
if we accept to descend into our misery
and there cry out to him.
Then he will answer, 'Here I am, Beloved,'
and will enfold us in his arms
with a long embrace.

It is such an incredible joy
to know that we are loved
with an unconditional love.
It is through our very wounds
that this love surges up within us.

It is then we discover
that *we* are the poor.
At l'Arche we might have come to serve the poor,
but we will only stay
if we discover that *we* are the poor,
and that Jesus came to announce the good news,
not to those who serve the poor,
but to those who *are* poor!
It is the broken ones who lead us
to our brokenness,
and to the knowledge that we need a healing saviour.
Thus they lead us to Jesus,
                    to healing,
                    to wholeness
                    to resurrection.

These two experiences –
of gentle communion and
of pain and darkness –
lead us thus, little by little, into covenant:
                    covenant with Jesus,
                    covenant with the poor.

Living in the Body of Community: Belonging

But these two experiences cannot be lived in truth
unless they are lived in community.
This community could be simply a group of people
bonded together through prayer and mutual support,
with a common vision in their love and concern for others;

or it might be a family
opening its doors to someone in need;
or a community specifically founded
to welcome those in pain and distress.
Without community
the experience of communion will lead quickly
to possessiveness
and using the other to fill our emptiness;
a tendency to manipulate this experience
to satisfy our own needs,
to respond to our own whims and desires.
An experience of love is *given*;
it can never be possessed;
it is a fleeting moment of eternity,
a gift of Jesus
that renews us.
How quickly though –
because of our brokenness and inner pain –
we seek to grasp, possess and preserve this gift.

Without community
the experience of inner pain and anguish
could lead us to hurt the weaker person,
as the powers of darkness are unleashed in each one of us
and we discover our capacity to undermine others,
to trample on them,
to hurt and crush them,
to break even further what is already broken.

Community provides the necessary safeguards and limits
but also the support
to allow us to live fully
these experiences of joy and pain.
Community gives the confirmation we need
to remain faithful.
It can provide also the challenge we need
to go forward,
so that we can live these experiences

as times of growth
on our pilgrimage,
which is both a journey to greater wisdom
and to the deeper rooting of our being.

Community is an experience of belonging and of solidarity,
as if people were born to be together.
For those who have encountered loneliness,
separation and brokenness
within their own family,
it is a deeply unifying and healing experience to be accepted,
just as they are,
    with all that they are (and are not!),
    with all that is broken, all the inner wounds,
    with all that is gift and light.

The sense of belonging takes time to be born.
We have to go through passages
that are more or less painful
before it comes to birth or reaches fulfilment.
For some it may come very quickly,
almost instantly,
as a gift of God to which they are called to be faithful.
For others it may take years.
There is often a strong resistance, not wanting to belong
or not wanting to believe
that we are called to be with others,
because to belong
means also to die to some aspects of our being:
    to our independence,
    to our freedom to do things.
In each of us there is a struggle against belonging.
We fear the call to claim and develop our gifts
to become responsible for others.
We fear also the call to submit to the gifts of others.
In each of us there is pride
that prevents us from believing

in the call and the promise of Jesus,
and from giving ourselves
in a love and humility
that would enable us to receive from others.

When we first begin to share our lives with others
there is a time of euphoria:
    a joy springing from deep within.
Everyone seems so wonderful,
we put them on a pedestal.
At last we have found a place where we belong,
after years of pain, searching and loneliness!
But then, when fatigue comes
or when we feel hurt, misunderstood,
unrecognized or put aside,
we begin to discover others as they are:
    a mixture of light and darkness,
        of love and hate,
        of trust and fear.
Then, in anger, we plunge them into the pit:
    they are all hypocrites!
    they say one thing and do another!
The discrepancy between word and life
becomes painfully apparent.
We lose trust.
The dream is over; reality is painful –
    not so much the reality of the broken people
    whom we came to serve,
    but the reality of those
    who have come to share their lives with them
    as followers of Jesus.

Like Peter in front of the littleness and brokenness of Jesus,
we cannot stand it.
The theories, dreams and illusions we had
about community, about humanity and about ourselves,
come crumbling down.
We are shattered.

In all of us there is a dream of a beautiful world
where everything is wonderful and whole.
There is a part of us that says
that brokenness is evil and should not exist:
there is a deep longing to return
to that original garden of paradise,
the Garden of Eden.
It is like the dream
that assumed or expected our parents to be perfect,
to be like God;
we were unable to see any flaws in them,
until the shattering day
when it seems the scales fell from our eyes
and all was revealed!
This dream flows from our insecurity.
As we touch our own brokenness
we want to live in a perfectly beautiful world,
      a perfectly beautiful community,
      a perfectly beautiful church.
Most of us have been repeatedly told
that we must be perfect;
we are not allowed to be weak and broken,
fragile and vulnerable.
So deep in our minds is this image of perfection
to which we must strive,
that we are led to deny
our own brokenness
and to despise the brokenness of others;
to condemn the community that is not perfect,
or does not correspond to our ideal.

The sense of belonging flows from trust:
trust is the gradual acceptance of others as they are
with their gifts and their limits,
each one with the call of Jesus.
And this leads to the realization
that the body of community is not perfectly whole
and cannot be,

that this is our human condition.
And it is all right for us
to be less than perfect.
We must not weep over our imperfections.
We are not judged for being defective.
Our God knows that in so many ways
we are lame and half-blind.
We will never win the olympics of humanity,
racing for perfection,
but we can walk together in hope,
celebrating that we are loved in our brokenness,
     helping each other,
     growing in trust,
     living in thanksgiving,
     learning to forgive,
     opening up to others,
     welcoming them,
and striving to bring peace and hope to our world.
So it is that we come to put down roots in community –
not because it is perfect and wonderful,
but because we believe that Jesus has called us together.
It is where we belong
and are called to grow and to serve.

It is then we truly learn that
community is a body;
that each one is a member of the body,
bonded together in a covenant
given by Jesus.
Each one of us has a place in the body;
no one is better than another.

St Paul tells us this in his letter to the people of Corinth:
     'We don't all have to be an eye or an ear or a foot!
     We must be ourselves,
     finding our unique place in the body.'
And he continues:

'Those parts of the body
which are most fragile and most indecent
are necessary
and should be honoured.'
The people who are the most broken,
the ones who are in great pain or anguish,
the littlest and the weakest ones
are at the heart of the community
and are a presence of Jesus – Jesus crucified and in pain.
The body is there to hold and to comfort them,
 to care for them,
  and to receive life from them.

Once we have discovered the mystery of covenant
and the community as a body,
many aspects of hierarchy, rivalry, competition
and the need to prove ourselves to be the best
begin to disappear.
Difference is no longer seen as a threat
but as a treasure.
True humanity is not based on hierarchy,
with the best on top
and the worst, the most ignorant on the bottom.
There is no perfect model.
There is no ideal person.
No one possesses all the gifts.
To be the leader is not a sign that one is the best,
the most popular;
superiors are not superior.
Humankind is called to know itself as one body.
And within the body of community,
or the body of the family,
each man and woman, old or young, must be respected,
each one recognized
for the value of their differences;
each one is needed to fulfil a unique role.

Then we can see the exercise of authority
as just one gift among many,
at the service of others.
Priesthood is another gift,
another way to offer oneself for the growth of all.

And at the heart,
at the very centre of the body of community,
there are the littlest, the weakest and the poorest,
bringing the gift of the presence of Jesus
as an icon,
as a sacrament.

As we experience community as a body
in which we have been called by Jesus
to belong to each other,
we discover that we are responsible for each others' growth
and for the development of each others' gifts.
We have the power to call forth the gifts of others
or to crush them.

We can only challenge the poor and the broken to growth,
and call them to be true in all things,
if the bonds of covenant and of trust
are deep,
and if we speak truly and humbly
and act out of love,
not fear or anger,
nor from a desire to control or dominate;
then we in turn can be open to be challenged
and called by the most broken
to growth and greater truth.

It is not easy to become part of the body of community.
To do it, we must die to ourselves,
        to our pride,
        to our need to do our own thing,
        and to our desire to be recognized as unique
        and all-important.

It is a struggle to give others their proper place,
free from judgement, condemnation or envy.
It is difficult to accept the differences of others
especially when their temperament, their make-up,
is totally different from ours.
Different types of people
seem to oppose or contradict each other.
Perhaps even more threatening
are those people who reflect back to us
those parts of our being we cannot face or accept.
They reveal to us
the brokenness that we deny in ourselves.
In a special way, they become our enemies.

Yet each one has his or her place in the body.
And Jesus calls us together to form one body,
to love one another as he loves us.
He calls us to live the miracle of love and of grace
which is community:
one body, one faith, one shepherd.
Not a community where everyone is the same,
not a community where there is fusion
   (which frequently means confusion),
but a community where, inevitably, on the human plane
and on the plane of our psyches,
there is tension and pain,
and feelings of dissatisfaction.
A community must be built on faith
and in the belief that we have been called into one body.

The very struggle to build community
is a gift of God
and in accepting it
we acknowledge it as a gift,
not received once and for all,
but one for which we must yearn and pray and labour
day after day.

Since community is a living, dynamic body,
it is in continual movement.
It evolves as people grow,
as the whole body grows in welcoming new people,
as other people leave and separate to create another body,
just as the cells of the body separate and multiply.
Each community, as well as each person,
lives its pains of growth,
its times of passage.

The danger for all of us
is to want a community that is strong and competent
with the security of wealth,
good administration and structures,
and experienced, competent, committed people.
None of us like to live in insecurity
in fear of tomorrow.
We are all like Peter,
afraid of walking on the waters.
So we can quickly close our hearts,
forgetting the call of Jesus
and how he brought us to life
through his guiding hand.

The gentle seed of love
at the birth of community
can so quickly harden.
It is not easy as community grows
to remain like children,
dependent upon our Lord and Good Shepherd
leading us to green pastures
and new forms of nourishment;
leading us,
as he led his people through the desert,
through new forms of poverty and insecurity.
There is the insecurity of a small prophetic community,
and there is the insecurity of a large, older community

with its structures
and long-term members,
some of whom have lost their inspiration.

Yet in our world
the poor and the weak
are always insecure,
at the mercy of human and political powers,
at the mercy even of their own brokenness
and inner violence.
We who are called by Jesus
to walk with them
and to enter a covenant with them,
are called too
to discover this road of insecurity,
where the power and wisdom of our gentle God
are revealed.

Yes, insecurity and weakness
are like a door
through which passes
the strength of God.
Do not flee then from insecurity;
do not seek to have all the answers.
If you do, you risk turning away from God
who is leading you into the Kingdom.

'The Lord gives power to the weary
and to the helpless ones he gives strength. . . .
Those who trust in the Lord
shall renew their strength.
They shall soar up with wings,
like eagles.
They shall run and not be weary;
they shall walk and never falter.'

If we are called to walk with the poor in community
Jesus will always be there,

saying: 'Do not be afraid,
        for I am with you.'

Forgiveness and the Bonds of Community

And it is true
that we continue to hurt one another.
We do not listen.
We lack compassion.
In spite of our deepest longings
we so quickly close ourselves up
and forget the call of Jesus.

Perhaps we put ourselves too much in the centre,
dominating in more or less subtle ways;
we crush and stifle people,
denying them their rightful position.
Or sometimes we are reluctant to acknowledge the place
that belongs to us,
Through timidity we hesitate to assert ourselves,
lacking confidence in ourselves and our gifts,
and thus we weaken the body
and allow or even force others to dominate too much.
The apportioning of responsibilities and relationships
in any community
is not static, fixed once and for all;
it is in continual flux as people grow,
and as they come and go.
And because nothing is ever perfectly established
it is easy to be hurt,
and to go on hurting others.

That is why all communities,
and this of course includes families,
must be built on forgiveness.

105

Forgiveness is the source and the rock
of those who share their lives:
    to forgive each day,
    to forgive and forgive and forgive,
    and to be forgiven just as many times . . .

Forgiveness is the cement that bonds us together:
it is the source of unity;
it is the quality of love;
that draws togetherness out of separation.

Forgiveness is understanding and holding
the pain of another;
it is compassion.

Forgiveness is the acceptance of our own brokenness,
yours and mine.

Forgiveness is letting go of unrealistic expectations of others
and of the desire that they be other than they are.

Forgiveness is liberating others to be themselves,
not making them feel guilty for what may have been.

Forgiveness is to help people flower, bear fruit,
and discover their own beauty.

Forgiveness does not need the drama of tears
and emotional hugging.
It is a simple gesture,
signifying that we are together, part of the one body,
called by Jesus
in a covenant with one another.

Forgiveness is peace-making:
struggling to create unity,
to build one body,
to heal the broken body of humanity.

Forgiveness is to follow Jesus,
to be like him,
for he came to give and to forgive,
to take from the shoulders of people
the yoke of guilt that locks them
into a prison of sadness and sterility,
and prevents them from flowing and living freely.

People who have suffered from rejection and deep insecurity –
especially as children –
carry within them a special and terrible form of guilt.
They feel that they are no good;
that nobody can love them.
This broken self-image incites them to anti-social behaviour
and acts of aggression or self-mutilation
that lead to even greater rejection.
It is a vicious circle of inner pain.
When they slap in the face
those who live with them,
they are testing them.
Their needs are infinite,
and when they are not satisfied
they get angry.
Their healing comes through a long process of encounters
drawing them to trust, love and fidelity;
a long process where they must feel forgiven,
not judged or condemned.
It is forgiveness repeated seven times seventy-seven times –
and even more –
that gradually transforms their fear into trust,
their negative self-image into one that is positive.
Then they in turn become capable of forgiving
those who hurt them when they were young.

Jesus came to teach us the way of forgiveness.
To the woman taken in adultery –
that woman who had broken the body of her family –
Jesus says: 'Neither do I condemn you;

go and sin no more.'
He looked at her and loved her with tenderness.
Her heart was healed
as she experienced this love of Jesus.
New life flowed within her,
and she became whole.
Jesus took from her the yoke of guilt.
He gave her new trust in herself.
She rose up to heal and rebuild her family.

Jesus tells of the prodigal son,
held in the arms of his father,
broken as he was.
He was tenderly embraced
and, being thus enfolded,
he was healed
and made whole.

Jesus came to forgive.
This is the secret of his mission,
teaching us also to forgive.
His cry on the cross: 'Father forgive them
        for they know not what they are doing!'
was also the cry at each moment of his life:
'Forgive.'
That is why he became the Lamb,
the Lamb of God,
to take away the sins of the world,
constantly forgiving.
He took into his flesh the violence of humanity,
        the accumulated violence of generations,
in order to transform it
into forgiveness and tenderness.
A forgiveness which is the experience of liberation:
        'Rise up!
        be yourself!
        bear fruit!

give life!
live the creativity of love
    in the body of community, of the Church
    in the Body of Christ.'

At the heart of the message of Jesus is his commandment:
    'Love your enemies;
    Do good to those who hate you.
    Pray for those who curse you.'

He points out that it is easy to love those who love us;
we do not need a special strength or love for that.
But by ourselves it is impossible to love our enemies.
Our natural instinct is to defend ourselves:
    either to attack or run away.
But with the gift of his Spirit,
Jesus leads us along the path of peace-making.

Before being a commandment,
the words of Jesus, 'Love your enemies,' are a promise:
'I will give you my spirit
to do what you cannot do by yourself.'
'I will teach you compassion,
    how to love and forgive those who hurt you,
        who criticize you behind your back,
        who limit your freedom,
        who prevent you from living,
        who reject you,
        who abandon you,
        who stifle you,
        who slap you in the face.'
With Jesus the impossible becomes possible.

Growing to Wholeness through Descent

In a special way,
for those of us called to live or work
with very broken people,
our purpose is to help them rise up
and discover and exercise their own gifts,
to discover their beauty and their capacity
to love and to serve.

The danger for those who are serving the poor
is to hold them back
by doing too much for them,
like parents who do too much
for their children with a handicap.
It is always easier to do things for people
than to help them find their human dignity, and self-respect,
by doing things for themselves.
When we *do* too much,
not helping others to grow
or take responsibility for themselves,
are we not just serving ourselves?
– seeking power and a pedestal?
To serve broken people
means helping them, like a mother helps her child,
to discover their own gifts and beauty,
helping them to a greater independence,
so that gradually we may disappear.

It means going down the ladder
and washing their feet
as Jesus did,
discovering the beatitude of littleness:
    to be hidden servants,
    taking the last place;
    it is there we find Jesus.
John the Baptist said that he must decrease
that Jesus might increase.

The power of God's glory grew only as Jesus disappeared,
descending to the lowest place.
Jesus said: 'It is good that I go,
    so that I can send you my Spirit;
    then you may grow
    and bear much fruit.'
And so, Jesus died on the cross,
and then hid himself in the bread of the Eucharist.
In the same way, those of us who are the strongest
or the elders in a community,
must learn to disappear,
    to take the last place,
    to become like bread,
so that others may be nourished and grow.

Mary in her song
tells us how God lifts up the poor
and takes the powerful down from their thrones.
In whatever way we come to share our lives
with the poor and the broken,
we are called to touch our own poverty and brokenness;
we are called to leave our thrones of power,
knowledge and security
to become little and humble.
There is no other way to fullness.
And at the same time as we enter
into relationship with the poor and the broken
they are called to rise up in hope and celebration.
This is the way of Jesus.
This is the way to be a peace-maker.
This is the path to unity.
To give the littlest and the poorest their rightful place,
not to isolate them in ghettos,
not to give them money,
but to give them their proper place in the body.

For some, who are perhaps seriously handicapped,
their place in the body
is simply to be the presence of Jesus,
        sacrament of Jesus,
        icon of Jesus,
        face of Jesus.
In their littleness
they have no voice,
but their bodies are the temple of the Holy Spirit.
Their unique role
is to be a home for Jesus and his Father,
        a secret, living tabernacle.
And they will only know this
if we reveal it to them,
        by the way we touch and bathe them,
        by the way we hold them,
        by the way we speak lovingly to them,
            even if they do not understand the words,
        by the way we are gently present to them,
        by the way we reverence them.

The disciples turned away from Jesus
        as he became powerless and vulnerable,
        excluded from the religious society,
        murdered outside the walls of the beloved city.
They could not accept a weak and weeping Messiah.
How can this man who falls help others to stand!

Let us pray that the Holy Spirit may enter our lives
wherever we may be
and teach us to be like Jesus,
to walk down the ladder
and discover the Saviour in the heart of the poor,
giving them their rightful position in society
and in the Church.

To walk with the poor is to go against the current of society.

To work for them – even to fight for their rights
and to raise them into the normality of our society –
can be part of a culture.
But simply to live with them,
    to share their lives
      or to create community with them
      and to celebrate with them
         is not!
Followers of Jesus are called to be counter-culture.
Generally, culture separates itself from the poor.
It encourages only
walking up the ladder
toward greater power and reputation.

Jesus goes against this culture;
He goes against the stream of what people seem to want.
That is why eventually he is rejected.
He is seen as a dangerous person.
In him there is a gentle revolution,
    changing all things,
    making all things new,
    announcing the Kingdom
        where the powerful are dethroned
        and the weak uplifted;
        where enemies are pardoned
        and barriers fall,
        where armaments are dismantled
        and people join together as one body,
           each person playing his or her part;
           without competition or rivalry,
           but with forgiveness,
           celebrating unity in love.

A New Strength

In order to walk with the poor
we need to find a new strength,
a new energy,
not from books and studies
or the need to prove something,
not even from natural generosity and the need to grow
nor from the desire to save the world,
but an energy which comes directly from God.
We must be reborn in love and in the Spirit.
We cannot live with the broken people of our world
and start to mend with them the broken body of humanity,
welcoming and accepting our own darkness,
unless we receive the seed of the Spirit of Jesus
and nourish that seed
so that it may grow,
both inside us and inside the body of which we are a part.
There are many forces opposing the growth of that seed,
many forces of hate,
seeking to separate, to shatter and to break.
There are many forces of seduction
that fragment people and prevent growth.
There are many enemies of truth and love,
protecting their power, greed and ill-gained wealth.
There are enemies of unity,
and the foremost is the Evil One himself.
Though many do not like to acknowledge his existence,
the devil is the one who breaks wholeness
trying to seduce,
> to separate people one from another,
> to divide and build barriers,
> to encourage violence, conflict and revenge,
> to put people on pedestals and create an elite,
> which will put others down.

Jesus came to bring together that which is broken.
He gives us his Spirit, the Holy Spirit,

so that we, like him, may become men and women of peace,
making whole the fragmented.
That is why to create bonds of love and truth
with broken people,
and thus to become peace-makers,
we need to nourish ourselves
with a new energy coming from God.
We need to nourish the seed of the Spirit
planted gently in the vulnerable earth of our being.
For we may get burnt out or be tempted to give up
if we do not recharge our batteries,
if we do not come to drink of the waters
flowing from Jesus:

> 'Let he who thirsts come to me to drink;
> he who believes in me, as Scripture says,
> rivers of living waters will flow from his belly.'

If we are not in communion with Jesus
we will not be able to give our lives and bear fruit.
To pray is essentially that:

> to come to Jesus and to drink,
> to come to him as to a friend,
> to be in communion with him,
> to remain in his love,
> to trust him,
> and to follow him;
> it is to rest in him.

To pray is to cry out to Jesus
and to the Paraclete,
the One who answers the cry,
when we cannot go on
or when we fall
and touch our pain and brokenness.
It is to offer all this pain and the pain of the world,
with him and in him,
to the Father.
It is to let the Holy Spirit penetrate into our brokenness

and lead us to wholeness
and teach us how to love as he loves.

Prayer is to be in contact with our own centre;
it is to be close to our own source;
it is to let Jesus make his home in us
and to make our home in him.
It is to be guided by Jesus, our good shepherd.

Jesus also gives us a special nourishment:
the bread of heaven,
       his body
       his blood.
He offers us this strange and wonderful nourishment
and he asks us to eat and drink humbly,
not understanding but trusting,
coming to the table like children,
hungry and thirsty,
terribly in need of food:
    'For he who eats my flesh and drinks my blood
    abides in me and I in him.'

When Jesus spoke of his body as food
and his blood as drink,
the people were shocked,
for they are outrageous words, meaningless, mad –
if we think about them only with our rational minds.

From that day on many disciples left him,
no longer able to walk with him,
for these words were too hard.
But if we accept these words through the eyes of love,
they become a promise and a secret,
showing us the desire and the passion in the heart of Christ:
    to live and love in us,
    to work through us,
    to signify his presence
        by bread transformed into his body.

116

The Eucharist is our daily bread,
given at the table of sacrifice, the altar of offering.
It is there, with Jesus, we can offer our own pain
and the pain of the world
to the Father.
It is there that sacrifice and communion,
pain and ecstasy,
the cross and the resurrection
become intimately woven
and become the centre of our lives
and of the community.

The broken bread, the broken body of Jesus,
draws us towards the rejected, the hurt, the poor.
In them and through them too our hearts are fed,
but sometimes in a painful way.
The secret of Jesus is that his call is the cry of the poor.
This call both attracts and disturbs.
It nourishes and breaks open our heart,
calling us to hope and trust.
If in the Spirit we try to answer that cry,
opening our arms and our vulnerable hearts,
a peace is given to us.

But we are also nourished by the Word of the Gospels
that gives new meaning to the world
and to the history of mankind.
This Word of God is food for the mind and the heart;
we need it.
Without it we can quickly fall under the influence
of that other vision
which pervades our world:
    a vision of power and reputation,
    pleasure and individual autonomy;
    a vision in which weakness is decried
    and fragile, vulnerable people are seen as useless;
    a vision whereby we must defend ourselves with force
    and seek wealth and security.

117

Without the nourishment of the Word of God
we tend to fall into a state of discouragement and guilt,
feeling helpless in front of the brokenness of the world
and prey to those mocking voices:
    'Be like everyone else!'
    'Why try to be special?'
    'Who do you think you are?'
We get seduced by riches and by power;
    by status and by superficial pleasures.
We begin to doubt
and thus tend to float along with the current.
The Word of God calls us back
    to belief in the communion of love,
    to presence,
    to the beatitudes announced by Jesus.
It gives a name to that secret peace
and that tender ecstasy
of which we have had only a glimpse.
It gives us the strength to accept pain
and to offer ourselves in sacrifice to the Father.

We are called daily by Jesus
to make an inner choice
and to become responsible
for our growth and our capacity to give life
and for the growth of others.
But we must make this choice
with the commitment of our whole life.
Do we really want to follow Jesus,
to answer his call,
to become peace-makers in this broken world of ours?

If we are to grow in love
and to become more fully men and women of peace
day after day,
we need a guide.
All alone we shall quickly become discouraged,
fall away,

and seek the more trodden path.
Without a guide
it is difficult to recognize the fruits
of the presence of God in our lives.
When we touch a point of pain,
we will panic and run away.
We need a wise and loving guide,
a follower of Jesus;
one who knows his ways
and the secret of his presence
in the poorest and the littlest of people;
who will remind us of the call of Jesus
and how he has been present in our lives,
gently guiding us at all times;
who will remind us that we are loved
and called to walk with Jesus
on the road of pain and compassion
in resurrection.
Such a guide will not tell us what to do,
but will listen and discern with us,
our way
in the Will of the Father.
The guide will be able to put a name to what we are living.
The guide will hold us in prayer, lovingly,
calling the Spirit upon us,
confirming us in our call,
challenging us too
and calling us to be true in all things.
This guide must be a man or woman of God,
perhaps a priest or minister,
one who deeply knows our humanity,
our own points of pain, weakness and growth,
as well as the tender, secret ways of God.

The one who is guide
can show us also the gift of the forgiveness of Jesus.
It is a beautiful and liberating thing
to find a guide and confessor

who can carry all our sins and weaknesses,
and to whom, as a gentle instrument of God's mercy,
we can open our hearts as to Jesus,
knowing that he will be compassionate.

Rhythms of Rest and Renewal

In order to grow towards wholeness,
accepting our brokenness
and gradually becoming more compassionate,
we need the power of the Spirit.
But we are humans
and must also know the ways of our own bodies and beings.
We must become wise.
Without human wisdom, inspired by God,
we will not attain wholeness
but will continue to live in some spiritual tension,
dream or idealism.
Rest, relaxation and discipline are important.
I am surprised, at l'Arche and elsewhere,
that many people do not know how to rest.
They are like rolling locomotives,
fuelled by anguish, and perhaps by the fear of stopping.
And when they do stop,
it is just to sleep more
or to potter around, not knowing what to do.
Each one of us must find our own secret rhythm
of how to rest, relax and find re-creation,
for each one of our bodies is different.
We need personal space and time.
God gave the Jewish people the Sabbath
as a day of rest.
Each one of us must discover our own sabbath,
our real nourishment.
This is all the more important
for those of us who are called to live with much tension

and to carry great stress.
This tension and stress
that we experience as we live with wounded people
can prevent growth and stimulate anger and exhaustion,
which are not always recognized and acknowledged.

We must learn
not just to free ourselves from tension and fatigue
on the sabbath day, our day of rest.
We must also learn,
as the mother must learn
in front of the never-ending needs of her children,
how to respect our energy
and relax in all the moments of our day
filled as they may be with arduous work
or often tiresome meetings,
and crises of all sorts,
and the hundred and one things-that-have-to-be-done.
To do this we must discover how to harmonize
the active and the passive in us.
If we are just doers,
feeling terribly responsible and serious,
we will crack up one day.
We must nourish the passive part of us,
our hearts made for a personal love,
learning to listen to others,
to marvel at nature,
to rest a moment in the presence of Jesus,
to receive the love of those around us
and be nourished by their trust,
enjoying the little things of each day,
not taking ourselves too seriously,
accepting to become like little children.

We have learnt at l'Arche that
celebrations, recreation and nourishment
are close to one another.
It is important to learn to celebrate:
celebrating the oneness of our body
as it moves towards healing and wholeness;
giving thanks together
in dance, mime, singing and laughter.
Yes, each feast should be truly a celebration,
a great and joyous celebration:
Christmas, Easter, holy days, anniversaries, birthdays,
beginnings and ends of the year,
special visitors.
There are so many occasions
for giving thanks and celebrating.

Meal times are important,
the meals of each day.
How important it is to eat well,
in laughter and gentle relaxation.
It is a moment when people come together
to be renewed.
Meals are not just for the stomach –
vital as it is that our physical body is fed and nourished.
Food is linked to love and to unity.
Every child sucking at its mother's breast
knows that as well as the mother.
It is by this love and unity
that meals become a time of renewal and celebration.

Jesus linked food and love in so intimate a way
at his last meal,
when he gave his broken body
signified by the broken bread
as food,
and invited us to take and eat.

As we discover the rhythm of life
which is also the rhythm of our bodies,
we can find inner harmony and gentle serenity.
The secret is to learn
    to be silent inwardly,
    to be full of gentle laughter and joyfulness,
    to be compassionate to all those who are in pain.

This harmony is a gift of God to us humans,
based on openness and welcome:
    to welcome Jesus,
    the tremendous Lover
    and the Lamb,
    in whom joy and pain are intermingled;
    to sing and laugh and rejoice
    in the beauty of God's creation.
Yes, it is true that God wants a joyful people,
but with our hearts open and welcoming
to those who are suffering.
This is compassion:
    offering our lives with them to the Father,
    hoping in the promise: 'Come, Lord Jesus, come!'
We are thirsting for the wedding feast
where all will be present
and where war and oppression,
conflict and pain
will be no more.

Our Searching Hearts

For many who come to live with the poor and the broken
there is a fundamental question in
their hearts about human love.
Should I seek a husband or a wife,
or am I called to celibacy?
Marriage is certainly a beautiful reality:

a wedding feast
a sacrament of God's love,
to love and be loved in a unique way;
a faithful companion always there
for me to cherish;
to make a home together
and to have children,
      the wonderment of motherhood and fatherhood.

But marriage, however beautiful,
is not just a honeymoon of love;
      it implies many deaths.
It implies fidelity to one person
and a caring for this companion.
It implies a constant love for the children
as they are,
and not as we dreamed they would be.

Jesus calls us to follow him
but he does not always make it clear
whether we are to walk alone or with another.
But if we put roots down with broken and little people
it becomes clearer.
We discover the fundamental meaning of our lives,
the call of Jesus.
We discover his secret
hidden in brokenness.
If then our way is defined by this meaning and this secret
we need not worry.
If God wants us to marry
and to live a particular relationship with one person,
he will show us,
and it will be in the context of the way
to which he has called us.
The companion will be the one who helps us
to live more fully the way of love and compassion,
to live more deeply the beatitudes,
to share more wholly in the healing of the broken body.

Before looking for this intimate relationship
it is important for every person to choose their way of life.
If we put a desire for intimacy with another
over and above the deepest call of our lives,
the relationship is in danger one day of breaking.
We must trust that in choosing our way
we will find the companion
who will share this way with us.
Then our intimacy will be strengthened
as we walk the same road together.

Some, whether they are at l'Arche
or in some other situation,
will gradually discover the call
to live celibacy in a positive way,
to live celibacy for Jesus.
Their hearts, their beings are for him,
trusting in his promise,
awaiting in hope the Wedding Feast.
They have been touched by the gentle hand of grace:
their hearts have been awakened to an inner love,
    a quiet ecstasy,
    God's embrace.
How can we speak of this mystery
except to say that it is gentle and sometimes painful.
Prayer and the Eucharist
take on then a new meaning;
and there is a new knowledge of the secret name of Jesus,
a name announced by John the Baptist:
    'Bridegroom',
    'Beloved'.
We discover that this tremendous lover touches us
in the depths of our loneliness,
as no human lover can touch us,
and calls us to the gentle fire and yearning of love,
to a peace that surpasses all peace.
There are no words
for the power and gentleness of this experience:

the heart of Jesus
in my heart.
Those who are called to this path are happy
to accept the pain of celibacy,
to be in solidarity with those with whom they live
and whose beings cry out from brokenness
for intimacy with another.
Many broken people, many people,
so deeply want this intimacy
but it is not possible or it does not happen.
They do not find the companion they long for.
Their beings cry out in pain and loneliness.
Community with its partial relationships
is not sufficient for them.
The wound is so deep.
But we can walk together,
and touch and love each other
and share the pain
and also the joys and the hope
of the eternal Wedding Feast!

The Body of Humanity and the Body of Christ

At l'Arche we are not alone in our struggle for peace
and our desire to live with broken people.
We are not the only followers of Jesus
who walk the downward path,
into the pains of the earth,
in the hope of rebirth and growth towards freedom.
All over the earth little communities in flower,
followers of Jesus
radiating light in so many places of pain:
    little lights shine in refugee camps in Cambodia,
    eyes of love and compassion

126

burn in the horror of our prisons,
faces of hope glow in the ghettos,
brothers and sisters, missionaries of charity,
close to those who are dying,
bathing them with love;
little sisters and brothers of Jesus,
close to the poor,
          discovering the beauty in them.

And in every parish too, in every home, in every heart
that welcomes a wounded person,
there is the quiet presence of Jesus,
consoling, loving, announcing the good news.
Yes, all over the world
the poor are discovering their value and their beauty:
the light of the world is present
in their bodies and their inmost being,
God is revealed.

Yes, over the earth and down through the generations
the light of hope is lit,
and it will never die out.
The flame is passed on
from people to people,
from heart to heart.
No political or military regime can extinguish it.
A Spirit is being given.
So we must take courage
when the tempest blows in our lives
and Jesus seems to be asleep.
For in other parts of the world
the sun is still shining,
and Jesus is more clearly present.

And there is a strange and mysterious link
between those people, all over the world,
who are yearning for the light to be incarnated,
in works of peace and justice and compassion,

encouraging each other in a secret, invisible way:
    those oppressed, crucified and in pain
    and those who are strong and in good health;
    those in quiet contemplation
    and those labouring arduously under the sun;
    those who love in silence
    and those announcing or receiving the good news.

As followers of Jesus,
we are all drinking
from the same unfathomable source.
We are all bathing
in the same life-giving waters.
These waters have flowed over generations,
springing from the wounded heart of Jesus;
gentle waters that flowed through the prophets of old.
Jewish prophets, Hindu prophets,
Buddhist prophets, Muslim prophets,
men and women of God
inviting us to the waters of rest and of life.

Since the day the Word became flesh
and became one among us,
each human being is intimately linked to Jesus.
The Word became man in every way:
a human, vulnerable heart
    with the capacity to love
    and the capacity to weep and to suffer pain,
    and so able to forgive and be compassionate.
Jesus is one of us, one of our flesh.
He is the elder brother of us all,
brother of the littlest and the weakest person
who may not even know him by name.
He is the lover of each man and woman,
for each one is the work of his hands,
each one is in the image of God,
each one has the light of God burning within him or her;
he cares for each one;

he yearns for each one to live and celebrate life.
And he says so clearly that
he is the hungry and the thirsty,
he is the person in prison or sick in hospital,
he is the stranger, the person lying naked in the street.
Here lies the mystery.
The body of Christ is humanity.

The Church is the assembly of believers,
those who have been called
out of a world full of sin and hate and fear,
but also to remain in it as a witness of love
and a sign of the resurrection.
The Church is those who trust in Jesus,
who recognize in him the Lamb of God
who saves and heals, and frees us from guilt.
But it is also a Church of pain,
because it is a Church of sinners
who believe and do not believe,
who trust and do not trust,
who walk in light but also in darkness.
The secret face of the Bride, the Body,
is full of light.
But the visible face of the Church is clouded.
Yet we should not be disturbed by the clouds;
there is sun shining behind them.

The Church must always announce with authority
the mind of Christ and speak out
against those who oppress or mislead the poor.
The Church must continually seek,
    through the signs and fruits of the Spirit,
    through the Word of God,
    through the writings of his holy ones, the saints,
    through the presence of the Spirit in the Church
        throughout the ages,
the message of Jesus and his ways.

But the Church must be careful
not to place yokes on people's shoulders
which are too heavy to bear.
The Church must evolve and change
according to the mind of the Spirit.
Sometimes this evolution is rather slow.
It is true that the boat seems sometimes so heavy laden
and the winds are not always fresh.
We would like it to move faster,
cruising over the troubled waters of humanity.

The Church is made up of ordinary human beings
with their grace and their limits.
Those who carry the burden of authority,
receiving the mandate to serve from Jesus,
must listen a great deal,
for they are at the service of the Body.
They carry the grace of their mission
but they too are wounded and fearful,
a mixture of light and darkness.

We can be impatient;
maybe Jesus too is impatient, but he waits.
O gentle Jesus,
how you wait for me as you wait for each one of us.
        For the pharisee,
                the sinner,
                        the mediocre and the fearful one,
                is also me.
Forgive me and help me to rise up
with greater lightness,
in the glorious liberty of the children of God.

If we who follow Jesus wish to share our lives
with broken people,
it is important that we are not just doing our own thing,
proving our goodness.
We are but a tiny cell of a vast Body, the Church.

She is a mother bringing us to birth,
feeding and teaching us.
We are part of this Body,
and this Body needs us.

The light shining in each of us
renders the Body more beautiful.
And we are called to love this Body
as it has grown over generations,
founded upon Jesus and his apostles
when the Spirit came upon them
      on the day of Pentecost.

And in the Body of the Church
there are many different members.
We are joined together in a gentle covenant
and communion:
      No one is better than the other.
      But each one is there for the others,
      shedding light one on another,
      each one in need of the other.

How much we need holy ministers, priests, bishops,
and the Pope,
loving, unifying, confirming, challenging,
announcing the good news,
giving us the Body of Jesus.

And many of us in our little communities of l'Arche
can give witness to the grace we have received
through men and women of prayer
hidden in various monasteries across the world,
rising in the night or early morn,
singing Jesus.
How much we need the prayers flowing from
      little people,
      sick people,

aged people,
secret contemplatives.
Prayers offered in the pain of their broken bodies
confined to wheel chairs or to their beds,
calling out to Jesus,
singing Jesus.

Communities must never be cut off one from another,
forming little ghettos of self-sufficiency,
wrapped up in their own affairs.
We must be busy like the bees,
going out from the hive, the community,
far and wide to scattered flowers,
each one uniquely giving glory to God.
We must join hands one with another.
We need each other.
We need to confirm
and encourage each other,
pray for each other.
Each one with their differences
and the uniqueness of their gifts,
each one with their own point of pain and infidelity
is beautiful.
Together we are like a source of water
flowing gently over a thirsty humanity.

The broken Body of the Church
is the source of so many tears.
Maybe today Christians are not fully one
in their beliefs, their organization and their structures.
But they can be one in their love
and in their yearning to follow Jesus,
not always knowing the path ahead,
which will be revealed little by little by the Spirit.
They can be one
as together they walk down the ladder with Jesus,
meeting Jesus in the poorest and the weakest.
It is true

that Christians cannot all eat today around the same table
of the broken bread,
transformed into the Body of Christ,
but they can eat together
around the same table
with the poor and the weak.
Is not this the most direct path to unity?

It is true that Christians of different traditions
cannot drink today from the same chalice
of the blood of Christ
but we can all drink together
from the same chalice of suffering:
    the sufferings of division
        of brokenness in our world.
Together we can pour the sweet oil of compassion
upon the wounds of humanity.
Unity will come
not only around the treasure of the body of Jesus,
    his broken, risen body
    hidden in the Eucharist
but also through the treasure of the broken body of Jesus
in the poor.

The Eucharist,
and the washing of the feet of wounded people,
the broken body of Christ,
are in some ways
the same reality:
one giving meaning to the other,
one flowing from the other.

Communities of Peace

My brother, my sister,
with Jesus you have been called

to be a bridge.
Maybe you have been called
to be a healer and a peace-maker,
to leave your own culture,
to enter into another culture,
the culture of the poor and of the broken.
Whatever your circumstances, the call is there,
to walk down the ladder
in surrender and trust,
to discover Jesus,
the light shining in the darkness.
You are called to reveal to people
their beauty,
their magnificent light,
their place in the heart of God.

If you are called to bridge the gap
between the rich and the poor
between cultures and nations
and to become a universal brother or sister,
wherever you may be,
you must strive for inner wholeness,
which is peace in yourself.
Deep within your own self
must come together
     your head
     your heart and
     your hands;
     your sexuality integrated into your being,
     and into your capacity to relate.
Deep within yourself,
your spirit and body must join more intimately together.
You are called to accept and integrate
your darkness and your brokenness,
letting the healing Spirit of Jesus
penetrate into those parts of your being
where you are so terribly vulnerable and even frightened.
He knows us so well,

for he is the Word who created us.
He alone can make all things new,
out of wisdom and love,
as the Creator.
It is only as you become whole,
as you accept your own brokenness and misery
and as you let the healing power and mercy of Jesus,
our Saviour,
descend upon you,
and rise within you,
that you will become a source of unity for others.
It is only if you discover your thirst
and drink of Jesus,
that you can flow over into others,
giving peace.

So let us open ourselves
to the healing, forgiving Spirit of Jesus.
Let us open up all the pains of the past,
the wounds that came from the moment of our conception
– wanted or unwanted –
and from the months we were carried
in our mother's womb;
the wounds from our early childhood
when we felt rejected
or stifled,
unloved in our being
and unrecognized in our gifts;
the wounds coming from all the failures of the past:
      our incapacity to love and give life,
the people we have hurt
because of our sinfulness, pride or fears, and the barriers
we have built around our vulnerability.

Let us allow the healing, forgiving Spirit of Jesus
to penetrate our whole being,
and lead us to wholeness.
Then will rise from that very darkness

a new compassion,
bonding us to others.

Peace-making does not begin
in big meetings or street marches,
but in welcoming with compassion
others with whom we live and share and work,
those who threaten us
because they are different;
those who hurt us,
'our enemies',
because they tread on our toes,
do not give us enough consideration
or the place we feel should be ours.

Peace-making begins at home
as we carry the wounds of others,
and allow them to carry ours,
in compassion,
uplifting them,
and nourishing their gifts.

In this way, a family or a community
is built up,
not founded on laws, administration or good organization
– necessary and important as these may be –
but gently developed through loving relationships.

But we must always remember
that the first peace-makers
are the broken people themselves:
    it is their cry of pain,
their cry for love,
the primal cry springing from their brokenness
which attracts and calls forth people,
but disturbs them too:
it both heals and hurts.

Jesus said: 'When I am lifted up
          then I will draw all to me.'
His wounded body,
the innocent lamb,
awakens in us
hearts of compassion and truth.

The child, the innocent child,
and the hungry, lonely beggar
closed in upon his despair,
carry in them a secret power
to attract people to them,
in compassion.
They bring people together
in love:
but they can be also a source of division and of fear,
because their cry is calling us to a change
we do not wish to make.

It is sometimes difficult
in communities which are small
and where only a few broken people seem to receive life
to believe that it all has meaning.
There is something in us all
which thinks that 'big is beautiful'.
We feel we must do big things,
strike at the source of evil and not the symptoms,
do good on a large scale
welcome and save more and more people,
organize things,
propagate a message all over the world,
write books,
speak on television.
But the more we do this,
the more we risk losing the essential,
uprooting ourselves from bonds of love;
thus we begin to die.

The basis of true human life
is a rooting in the earth,
faithful relationships,
fidelity to those to whom we are bonded in love,
carrying one another's burdens,
sharing with them their joy and their pain.
It is compassion and forgiveness.
Small is truly beautiful.
Jesus spent thirty gentle, loving years
with Joseph and Mary,
teaching us about rooting, about a sense of belonging,
and forming community.
Nazareth is our school of life,
teaching us
    to live humbly in the presence of God,
    to work with our hands,
    to welcome people as they are
        with their gifts and their hurts,
    to walk in truth,
    to open our hearts to people and to nature.

And it will be from there,
from fidelity and love
for those with whom we are called to live,
that we might be called to stand firm
against insolent might and power structures;
called also to the struggle
to help each person find
their rightful place in society and in the Church,
and the space in which to grow.
It will be from there that each of us,
according to our call and our gift,
will become an agent of change and of love
for the whole of society.

It is true that some people are called to govern

and do things on a larger scale,
to make laws that are just.
Some are called to create jobs;
others must work in healing and in social professions;
still others teach.
All are necessary.
A society is composed of many people,
with many roles.
But in all these roles
the same principle applies:
small is beautiful.
We must create situations and communities
where each person
– especially the poorest and the weakest –
can attain human dignity,
find fulfilling work and the warmth of family life
and rejoice in the good news of Jesus.

This is the vocation of us all:
    to live real and loving relationships,
    to be peace-makers,
creating and recreating the body of community.

St Paul, in his letter to the Corinthians,
tells us that if we do big and beautiful things
    and speak with all the tongues of angels and of people,
    have all knowledge
    and even a faith to move mountains
    and have not love,
    then we are nothing.

Then he goes on to explain:
'Love is being patient and kind,
    not jealous or boastful,
    not arrogant or rude.
    Love does not insist on its own way;
    it is not irritable.
    Love finds its joy in truth.

Love bears all things,
believes all things,
hopes all things,
endures all things.'
Yes, love is manifested in the small things
concerned with another person.

And in all of this,
our model is Joseph, Mary and Jesus
in Nazareth.
They teach us what it means
to be human.

Some get discouraged,
because everything seems so small and so insignificant:
living all the time,
perhaps, as at l'Arche,
with the same few people who have a mental handicap.
The results are not very impressive.
Living in this way becomes possible
only if we discover the contemplative aspect of our lives.
To live in the presence of Jesus
and in the presence of broken people,
desiring to be a sign of love.
To believe that in all that littleness,
we can give joy and glory to the Father
and be in him an agent of change.

Maybe the very fact that we struggle
to recreate the body,
the body of community,
and that we live with people
very different from one another
and from ourselves –
people who belong to different churches or religions
or have none,
people from different races, cultures, classes –
is a sign that difference can become a treasure,

that war is not inevitable;
peace and unity are possible
because of a love that flows from the broken one,
Jesus,
who carries for eternity,
in his glorious body,
the wounds inflicted upon him.

Perhaps we can be a sign
of the value of each person,
no matter how broken,
no matter how poor
or how apparently useless he or she may appear to society.
A sign that they carry a treasure in their hearts.

Perhaps through our struggle to save and help
one person to find freedom
we are struggling for all humanity
and all the oppressed.

Perhaps we can help reveal the secret of the gospels:
    that God chooses what is foolish
    in order to confound the wise;
    that God chooses what is weak
    in order to confound the strong;
    that God chooses what is lowest and most despised
    to reveal his power and glory.

Thus we can help to call forth others
to walk on the downward path,
the path of humility and compassion,
so that people may discover for themselves
the saving power of the gospels:

    Jesus, the Lamb,
    who comes to bring peace to the world
    by taking away sin
    and opening our hearts to the poor and the broken,

so that together we can celebrate our oneness
and grow to freedom.
For the glory of God
in the wholeness of his Body
is each human person fully alive.

Epilogue

I began this book
in the quiet of a Trappist monastery,
enfolded by the prayers of the monks.
I am finishing it in Bethany,
on the West Bank,
a few miles from Jerusalem.

Bethany was a place of rest
for Jesus.
He liked to go there to rest
with Martha, Mary and Lazarus.

Today Bethany is a place of unrest,
a place of tension.
During this short visit
I have witnessed so much pain
throughout the West Bank of the river Jordan.
The University of Bethlehem is closed by the military;
students have been shot and killed.
There is anger, fear
and a feeling of desperation.
In the old city
houses belonging to Arabs have been burnt down.

We have started a small community in Bethany,
in the Muslim area,
near the desert which leads to Jericho.
There we have welcomed Ghadir,
a fourteen-year-old girl,
whose body is twisted and crumpled
and whose eyes are dark and serious:
her gentle face moves from apathy or sadness
or simply tiredness

to a brilliance of peace.
Her smile lights up her whole being
as she says gently,
'I love you'.
She has few words
but they are words of love.
Yes, from her weakness
flows a radiance of love.
She is a little flower
which can be easily crushed
under the boots of political and military power.

Ghadir is Muslim.
Her parents are poor and overburdened.
Our neighbours are also Muslim:
Ali and Fatma with their seven children
live above us.
They are the owners of our apartment.
They are friends;
they protect and help us
and give us their love.

While all around us there are troops,
causing both fear and violence,
and struggles for power, bringing hatred and mistrust,
the smile of Ghadir
flowing from the weakness of her body
is a light in the world,
is a light for the world.

My brother, my sister,
like Abraham
you also have been called to leave your family and friends,
to be a bridge
in a world of division and war.

You too are called to meet,
in the face of Ghadir and others like her,

the gentle presence of God.
You too are called to be
a man or woman of peace.

Remember the call of Jesus
who draws you out of the world of comfort and security
so that you may walk with him
and with the Ghadirs of this world.

There will be times
when you feel insecure and overpowered,
pulled into doubt and confusion.
Remember the gentle call of love
of Jesus and of Ghadir:
    'Come follow me.
    Come and be with me.
    Do not be afraid.
    I will be your strength and your security,
        your source of hope.'

Bethany,
December 1986